THE
HEALING
JOURNEY
THROUGH DIVORCE

Your Journal of
Understanding and Renewal

Phil Rich, EdD, MSW
Lita Linzer Schwartz, PhD

John Wiley & Sons, Inc.

NEW YORK ✦ CHICHESTER ✦ WEINHEIM ✦ BRISBANE ✦ SINGAPORE ✦ TORONTO

This publication is designed to provide accurate and authoritative information in regard to the subject matter covered. It is sold with the understanding that the publisher is not engaged in rendering professional services. If legal, accounting, medical, psychological or any other expert assistance is required, the services of a competent professional person should be sought.

Library of Congress Cataloging-in-Publication Data:
Rich, Phil.
    The healing journey through divorce : your journal of understanding and renewal / Phil Rich and Lita Linzer Schwartz.
        p.   cm.
    Includes bibliographical references.
    ISBN 0-471-29575-2 (pbk. : alk. paper)
        1. Divorce.   2. Divorce—Psychological aspects.
3. Diaries—Authorship—Psychological aspects.
4. Diaries—Therapeutic use.   I. Schwartz, Lita Linzer.
II. Title.
    HQ814.R53   1998
    306.89—dc21   98-35238
                                                          CIP

Printed in the United States of America.

10 9 8 7 6 5 4 3 2 1

Contents

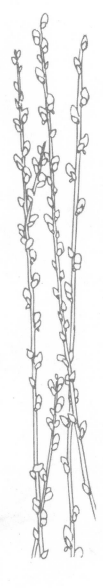

About *The Healing Journey Through Divorce*

YOU'VE BEEN HIT with a reality faced by millions of people each year. You or your spouse, or perhaps both of you, want a divorce. This decision changes your life dramatically. It is a shock wave that will be felt for many years to come. In virtually every case, divorce produces powerful emotions ranging from confusion to a sense of disorientation and loss. What can you do to understand and cope with your feelings? How can you address and ease the pain of personal loss? How do you proceed from this point on?

The Healing Journey Through Divorce is a not a book about the divorce process. Rather, it is a guided personal journal that will help you understand your feelings and work through the emotional and practical difficulties you'll face during your divorce. You will find a place to express your thoughts and discover answers as you regain footing along your life journey. Whatever the circumstances of your divorce—whether you're in the first throes, the final stages, or your divorce is long past—it will be important to work through its effects on your life and its impact on your feelings, thoughts, behaviors, and self-esteem. Your journal can be a valuable record of your life at this difficult time and can help you find ways to rebuild and strengthen your new life.

Not every "married" couple is legally wedded. There are many couples who are committed to one another and living together with intertwined lives but who are not technically or legally married. Sometimes these relationships are referred to as "common law" marriages, other times we simply say people are living together. Sometimes there are children in these relationships, sometimes not. Increasingly, society is moving toward treating partners who live together in committed relationships on par with legally married couples, regardless of whether the couple is in a heterosexual or same-sex relationship. Often these relationships are indistinguishable from legally wedded partnerships, and the emotional and practical commitments are just as strong. In any committed relationship that's breaking apart, the same issues are present regardless of the legal standing of the relationship. For this reason, *The Healing Journey Through Divorce* is as pertinent to the non-wedded couple going through a separation and breakup as it is to the legally married couple.

I

Embarking on Your Journey

WHEN YOU'RE CONFRONTED with legal separation, it may seem as though your whole life, not just your marriage, is falling into a chasm, especially if you're not the one choosing the separation. The future stops existing, and only emptiness looms ahead. In some cases, the initial separation turns around, problems are resolved, and the marriage continues. But for those where reconciliation is not possible—or desirable—separation is permanent and ultimately leads to divorce.

Divorce legally marks the close of a relationship. For some, the feelings evoked by a divorce and the issues that surround it pass relatively quickly. For others, the anguish and consequences last for years. Although often accompanied by grief, the goal of divorce work is not to bereave the marriage and analyze what went wrong but instead to accept, adjust, and move on as quickly as possible in the most emotionally healthy way.

Divorce Work

Divorce is composed of both *technical* and *emotional* aspects. The technical aspects will be taken care of one way or another—to the advantage, disadvantage, or mutual satisfaction of both part-

ners in the marriage—by the legal process. Although legal and social mechanisms exist for ending and separating the tangible aspects of marriage, little can be done to prevent the emotional storm that follows. In fact, the legal process may stir up even more emotions for you. The technical aspect of "divorce work," as handled by the legal system, is to ensure equity and the legal separation of partners.

The other side of divorce work concerns the emotional aftermath. Regardless of the circumstances of a divorce or the conditions that led up to it, the basis for any divorce work is understanding that the breakup of a marriage is a *loss*. It represents the ending of a romance and the failure of a partnership. Wherever you are in the divorce process, your divorce work is to deal with and work through the sense of loss, emotions, and situations caused by the divorce. Writing in a journal will give you a way to collect your thoughts and provide you with a tool to reflect upon and interpret your feelings.

Impact of the Divorce

The impact of divorce should not be underestimated. Despite living in a culture where the breakdown of marriages is commonplace and divorce an accepted occurrence, marriage is still sacrosanct. Marriages remain symbols and couples still build their lives around their partnerships.

As a result, for many the decision of one spouse to seek a divorce often comes as a shock to the other. If you're not the partner who first said "I want a divorce," more than likely you were initially shocked by your spouse's statement, and feelings of hurt, anger, grief, depression, and anxiety quickly followed. Perhaps you were even mystified by the strength of your spouse's decision. Alternatively, if you were the one who decided on this course of action, or the decision to divorce is mutual, the impact may be less shocking but just as significant, life changing, and emotionally numbing.

For many, divorce is a new experience. For others, marriage and divorce occur more than once. But it would be a mistake to assume that just because someone has been divorced that he or she is well equipped to handle any future failures of marriage. In fact, although a person may be better informed, more savvy, and seemingly better able to handle the practicalities of a breakup, a second (or more) divorce may be even more emotionally traumatic than a first.

Following the decision to divorce, you may be grief stricken; anxious about how you'll live from now on; and perhaps angry, guilty, depressed, or all three. You most likely will feel apprehensive about having to handle many of the day-to-day tasks of living alone with which you may have little or no experience or may have taken for granted. And you will have an ex-spouse who probably will cross your path frequently in the months immediately following the decision to divorce—and perhaps well beyond that especially if children are involved. This contact may take the wounds of the divorce longer to heal or hinder your ability to move on with a new life.

Following the decision to divorce, you may be grief stricken; anxious about how you'll live from now on; and perhaps angry, guilty, depressed, or all three.

Sharing Your Experiences and Getting Help

Divorce work is difficult. It involves loss, change, and fluctuations in self-esteem—a powerful combination of forces. The act of writing about and exploring your painful feelings may be uncomfortable. Some entries in *The Healing Journey Through Divorce* may evoke difficult and painful feelings, which may make you feel vulnerable. Seek help whenever you find yourself feeling especially pained, fragile, or lost. A support network of family and friends is important during your divorce work, but even so this might not be enough. If you find the emotional process especially difficult to bear, seek help from a therapist, divorce counselor, trained clergy, or divorce support group. Under any circumstances, if you're concerned about the legal and practical issues, seek out an experienced divorce attorney or mediator.

Moving Through *The Healing Journey Through Divorce*

If you're working with a divorce counselor or therapist, she or he may assign a specific chapter or journal entry for you. If you're working on your own, where should you start? Although *The Healing Journey Through Divorce* was designed to be used in the order presented, it may not always be possible or desirable to move in this sequence. For instance, you may come to an entry that you aren't ready for. If so, skip it and come back to that entry at a later date. You may also want to move in a different sequence because of an immediate need to deal with pressing emotional or life issues. For these reasons, each chapter and journal entry in this book can stand on its own, and you can pick the order best suited to your needs.

Although you may feel as though your world is completely falling apart, it is important to consider which of your needs and problems is most pressing. The next chapter, "A Road Map Through Divorce," will help you assess where you are in your divorce work and help you pick the best place to begin your work. Bear in mind that there are at least two aspects of any divorce that may require early attention. These are the legal repercussions and processes inherent in many divorces and the issues that pertain directly to the children of divorcing parents. These issues aren't addressed until Chapters 7 and 8, but if you have immediate concerns about either of these topics you may want to turn directly to those chapters after completing Chapter 2.

In general, it's a good idea to glance through *The Healing Journey Through Divorce* so you're familiar with its format and ideas, but don't rush through it. Just as you can't recover from the impact of divorce overnight, you shouldn't try to complete your journal in a few days. Consider working through one chapter at a time, staying with it until you've completed all the relevant journal entries in that chapter. This will give you time to reread and reflect on what you've written, before moving on to the next aspect of your divorce work.

Making Yourself Comfortable

You may or may not be used to keeping a diary or journal and perhaps feel unsure of how best to start. First, regardless of which chapter or entry you start with, you need to decide which conditions and environment will best support your journal writing. Here are some suggestions that may make the process more comfortable and productive for you.

- Set aside a regular schedule for working through your journal, preferably at a time of day when you're fresh and have the most energy.

- Take breaks during your writing if you need to. Stretching your legs can also give your mind a break.

- Consider playing some quiet music or other relaxing background sounds.

- Make sure you have pens and other writing instruments that are comfortable for you to use as you write.

- Pick a place to read and write that will be physically comfortable for you.

- Pick a place to read and write that will be emotionally comfortable for you as well. Do you prefer a quiet private location or a public community area?

- If writing is emotionally difficult for you, or you find your feelings or thoughts overwhelming at times, consider having a comforting picture or object nearby or something else that might be familiar and emotionally safe.

- Make sure there's someone available for you to talk to after you write, if you think you may need some personal contact or support.

- Once you've completed an entry, reread it. Reflecting on what you've written can help you gain new insights.

Set aside a regular schedule for working through your journal, preferably at a time of day when you're fresh and have the most energy.

Using the Entries

There is limited writing space available in *The Healing Journey Through Divorce*, and each entry is provided only once. But there are some entry formats that you'll want to repeat more than once. Feel free to keep a supplemental journal in addition to this book, where you can add your "spillover" thoughts or write additional entries. You may also want to photocopy certain blank entries in order to complete them more than once.

Each journal entry concludes with "Things to Think About," a series of questions for you to consider after you've completed your entry. These are not a formal part of the entry but are reflective points that may spark a further journal entry, serve as discussion points if you're sharing your divorce experience with a friend or counselor, or simply act as a focal point for your thoughts.

The Value of Your Journal

Much of the benefit of *The Healing Journey Through Divorce* comes from gaining skills in reflection and self-expression. As you answer questions or write your thoughts in a journal entry, you're having a "conversation" with yourself. Even if you have a problem expressing your thoughts and feelings to others, writing can be cathartic, allowing you to unburden yourself in private. The main thing is that you *are* expressing what you think and feel.

If you use your journal on a regular basis, it will be an important tool in your healing journey. As with so many other things in life, the value of an activity depends on what you put into it.

2

A Road Map
Through Divorce

TOM

I feel like I've been knocked off my feet. I thought our marriage was a good one and that we had a relatively happy family. I knew we had problems, of course, but I thought we were committed to each other until Carol told me she wanted a divorce.

That completely threw me, and I don't really know what to do now. Should I fight to save our marriage, or do I support her in getting a divorce if she's that unhappy? And then what? What will happen to my relationship with the kids, and how can I give up living with them? Should I give up living with them? How can I afford to support two households? And, what about that? If I move out, is that like abandoning the family, or is it just respectful of Carol's wishes?

I don't even know why she wants a divorce. Is it me, or is it another guy? I've got a hundred thoughts running through my head, all at the same time. I really feel lost here, and, of course, I can't talk to Carol about it. Does she have a lawyer, and should I get one? What will our friends and family say? What's my first step, and what's the right thing to do for everyone? I just never pictured that this could happen. I can't even begin to describe my feelings, other than miserable and scared.

7

THE HALLMARK OF marriage is the expectation at the outset that this will be a permanent relationship, one in which both partners commit their lives to one another and join their individual lives together forever. Accordingly, the breakup of such a relationship can be devastating and life disrupting, regardless of whether a couple is legally married or living together in a committed relationship.

However, many of the features of a legal marriage that need to be *legally* undone through the divorce process do not need to be undone when a common law marriage breaks apart. Nevertheless, with growing recognition of the rights of both partners in unwedded relationships, and the increasing tendencies toward litigation in general, there can be as many legal issues involved in the separation of a common law marriage, especially when children are involved. And the emotional issues in the separation of an unwedded couple are just as penetrating and devastating as a wedded couple. In fact, the issues faced by an unmarried couple going through a separation may be even greater, because without the legal protections offered by the institution of marriage the unmarried couple may have to be even more litigious to get their needs met.

Two Sides of Divorce

At this difficult time in your life, it can help to understand what's typical in the divorce process and what to expect from your emotions as your divorce progresses through the final decree and beyond. Recognizing which phase you're in and identifying where you are *now* is the first step toward healing.

There are a number of ways to describe what people pass through from the first announcement of a divorce to the point at which they're able to move on with their new lives, free of old emotional bonds. But there are two parallel processes of divorce that actively affect one another: the *legal* route to dissolution of the marriage and the *emotional* roller coaster that you're no doubt already on. Although these two aspects of divorce are separate, they're happening at the same time in different arenas of your life and each clearly and definitely influences the other.

The legal route results in the eventual court decree and involves attorneys, paperwork, financial settlements, judgments, and more. The divorce settlement usually follows a straight-line process to the eventual outcome. There are many self-help books that can instruct and guide you through that aspect of the divorce process. In all cases you're advised to secure adequate legal representation or other professional help from those who deal with the technical and legal aspects of divorce.

The Healing Journey Through Divorce focuses only on the emotional process of divorce. Similar to the legal side of the divorce process, there's a predictable sequence of feelings and events that you'll experience, as well as tasks you'll need to face to successfully deal with those experiences. Unlike the technical side, however, you can't resolve your feelings in a straightforward manner. Feelings fluctuate, and one can quickly be replaced by another. Anger might be replaced by sadness or guilt, only to return again later. Just when you think you're past one set of feelings—like feeling betrayed or let down by your ex-spouse—you might unexpectedly experience a resurgence of that feeling after seeing your ex-partner at a school meeting, family gathering, or at the mall.

Although the experience varies from person to person, it's typical for the newly divorced to confront these feelings for one to three years. They're the normal feelings associated with the end of one of the most important relationships of your life. But despite the constant turbulence felt during the postdivorce years, divorced people do go through stages as they pass through the legal and emotional processes of divorce. *The Healing Journey Through Divorce* can assist you in dealing with the emotional aspects of your divorce work, which include:

+ facing the reality of the divorce
+ working through painful feelings

There are two parallel processes of divorce that actively affect one another: the legal route to dissolution of marriage and the emotional roller coaster.

- experiencing the full range of emotions associated with the breakdown of your marriage
- coping with the situational and lifestyle changes resulting from your loss
- adapting to the change and reconfiguring your life

Emotional and Practical Stages of Divorce

Although everyone's experience with divorce is different, you can expect to go through four distinct stages, which combine an emotional reality that begins with the announcement of divorce and continues through the practical considerations that follow your separation.

Still, there's no precise measure of how long it will take to pass through these stages. Generally, you can expect your life to resume a course of its own within one to three years, but this can vary widely. For some, the legal divorce proceedings can drag on for years, drawn out by multiple legal maneuvers and court appearances and fueled by emotional, child custody, or financial issues. For others, the legal aspects of the divorce are finalized within months. Often, it's the emotional underpinnings of the divorce that determine the ease with which the marriage is legally ended and ties formally severed.

But there's no correct formula to tell you when you should feel a particular way or when you should stop feeling that way. The idea of emotional divorce work is for you to understand and stay on top of your emotions so that your brain, not your feelings, shapes the path of your divorce and your life.

The first stage of the divorce typically passes the most quickly. It's the quick hit and sometimes numbing shock wave as you realize your marriage is over. The second and third stages are the most active and represent the bulk of your active divorce work —these stages cover the most active legal, practical, and emotional changes in your life after divorce. Probably most of the issues raised by and about the divorce are going to be hammered

Although everyone's experience with divorce is different, you can expect to go through four distinct stages, which combine an emotional reality that begins with the announcement of divorce and continues through the practical considerations that follow your separation.

home, addressed, and worked through during these two stages. The fourth and final stage represents that time in your life during which you're moving away from the divorce and toward your new life. This stage really has no formal "end," but is marked by your full acceptance of the divorce and a resolution of most of the practical and emotional issues. It's also characterized by your recognition that you're capable of having a life outside of the former marriage and your ability to move forward with that life.

Four Stages of Divorce

STAGE 1: SHOCK AND DISBELIEF

Stage 1 begins as soon as the idea of a separation and divorce is introduced and sinks in. Sometimes during this stage people don't really believe the marriage is over (and, of course, sometimes this is true and reconciliation follows). But the emotional work of this stage can't really begin until you accept the reality of the separation. If you choose to believe that your marriage isn't really over or that this is just a phase that your partner is going through, then you're in a state of "suspended disbelief," and your life is frozen as you wait for it to return to "normal." The first announcement of divorce begins the first stage and involves four major tasks and issues that need to be worked through.

1. *Facing reality.* One of you, possibly your spouse, has announced the intention to separate and get a divorce. The first task is to come to grips with what's just happened.

2. *Self-esteem.* Feelings of inadequacy and even shame may creep in as you begin to question what *you* did wrong. The task is to confront how you see yourself and learn to bolster your self-esteem.

3. *Telling the world.* This task directly follows from your coping with issues about self-esteem and shame and helps you let others—family, coworkers, and friends—know what's happened.

4. *Getting support and help.* Many practical obstacles and challenges will suddenly appear as separation looms. Here, the task involves getting the emotional support and practical help you need from friends, family, and others who are part of your life.

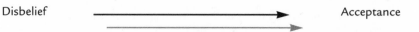

Disbelief   Acceptance

As you work your way through Stage 1, you'll pass from feelings of initial disbelief to a point of acceptance. You still may not believe that things are final, and perhaps you continue to hope for reconciliation, but if you're successful in dealing with the issues and tasks of the first stage, you'll reach a point where you can accept the facts of your situation and begin to actively plan your new life.

STAGE 2: INITIAL ADJUSTMENT

Stage 2 involves your ability to adapt to this new phase of your life. The initial shock has passed, and as the numbness wears off you start to feel the pain and begin to squarely face the many real changes that are part of your life now. The primary goal in this stage is adaptation and mustering the personal resources you'll need to manage the many emotional and practical changes you're going through. Four major tasks of Stage 2 include:

1. *Functioning and responsibility.* It's important that you continue to function effectively, appropriately, and responsibly during this very difficult and critical time in your life (e.g., meeting commitments).

2. *Confronting practical reality.* Adjustment involves attending to practical matters—where you live, financial stability, child care, and so on. Initial adaptation means ensuring a stable base for you or your children as you tend to the immediate and longer-term emotional, legal, and practical tasks.

3. *Addressing legal matters.* Even if you have a completely amiable divorce, you still must sever legal ties and the mar-

riage. During this early stage, you will be involved in the first steps of your legal divorce. This will likely include your search for or initial interactions with an attorney if you don't already have one.

4. *Managing emotions.* Throughout this stage you most likely will be inundated with powerful feelings of all kinds, from the self-esteem and shame issues of Stage 1 to feelings of anger, betrayal, and revenge. Your primary task involves finding ways to cope so that you're not swept away or overcome by your emotions. At this time you may decide to seek out help from a counselor for yourself or your children, if you or they are experiencing emotional difficulties.

Adjustment   ⟶   Acclimation

Stage 2 ends with your acclimation to the situation—your ability to live your new life, even though you may not like or even accept it. Neither adjustment nor acclimation signify your ability to control your emotions, nor do they mean that you're on top of things, but successfully working through these tasks does mean you've accomplished a great deal and have laid the foundation for the work ahead.

STAGE 3: ACTIVE REORGANIZATION

Stage 3 concerns include how you're living your life and how you're coping with the tasks of suddenly being single or a single parent; your tasks involve redefining yourself, your family, and your life. By now you've become aware of some of the enduring changes that you'll have to make (or have already made), and you're addressing these issues. Many of the issues and tasks you'll face during this stage involve:

1. *Managing lifestyle issues and practical affairs.* This stage covers issues that surround how you live your life and manage your affairs. It may involve moving to a new home, chang-

The beginning of the third stage is marked by the consolidation of your resources. . . . By the end of Stage 3, your life is more defined, and things are beginning to fall into place.

ing locks on your home, or choosing permanent child-care arrangements.

2. *Redefining relationships.* By now you have discovered those people you can count on and those who have moved away from active involvement in your life. In this stage you will more clearly define your relationships with people from your past married life, including your ex-spouse and former in-laws.

3. *Reconstructing personal values and beliefs.* The issues raised in this stage will make you evaluate yourself, what you want and what you don't want, what's important in your life, and how to find meaning in your postmarried life.

4. *Concluding legal procedures.* This stage is the most active element of the legal divorce process. How you handle this stage will affect child custody, finances, and the splitting of shared property as well as emotional outcomes for both yourself and any involved children.

Consolidation   ——————————▶   Definition

The beginning of the third stage is marked by the consolidation of your resources. Your life is physically more settled; you know what's available to you and what isn't. Even though emotional, practical, legal, and lifestyle issues are far from resolved, your life has taken a clear direction. By the end of Stage 3, your life is more defined, and things are beginning to fall into place.

STAGE 4: LIFE RE-FORMATION

Stage 4 represents the final steps as you pass through to the "other" side of your divorce. The worst is now behind you, and you have the opportunity to build a new life. In this final stage you'll deal with the emotional issues and life choices involved with squarely moving on with your life. The four tasks associated with this stage include:

1. *Constructing relationships.* As you move onwards, you'll not only redefine and rebuild old and existing relationships but

also construct new ones. These may be platonic, romantic, work related, or social in some other way.

2. *Developing new interests.* You have the chance to explore new interests or revisit old ones that were perhaps not viable in the past. These interests, like new relationships, provide part of the foundation upon which your postmarried life will be built.

3. *Accepting personal responsibility.* As you work through this final stage, you'll come to terms with the fact that you're fully responsible for your own life—for your emotional and physical health, your finances, your social relationships, and your choices. Where you go will be up to you.

4. *Accepting your new life.* In successful emotional divorce work, you finally reach the point where you're able to fully acknowledge and accept that your marriage is over and that you have a new life.

Clarification ⟶ Self-Direction

Stage 4 is characterized by clarifying the way things are as you enter the final stage in your divorce work. Much of the work in fully defining your relationship with your ex-spouse has been accomplished. The successful end point to Stage 4 is your ability to set the pace for your own life, wherever it may take you.

Moving Through the Stages

If you aren't moving through these stages as quickly as you think you ought to be or you feel stuck at one point—emotionally, legally, or spiritually—seek some help from friends or family. If you still feel stuck, seek professional help. For emotional and spiritual needs, consider a therapist or clergy. For legal matters, consult an attorney with expertise in divorce or someone skilled in divorce mediation or arbitration.

CHECKPOINT: STAGES

Circle the letter that best describes where you are *right now* with each task.

Stage 1 Tasks	I can't deal with this task.	I'm working on this task.	I've completed this task.
Facing reality	A	B	C
Dealing with self-esteem issues	A	B	C
Telling the world	A	B	C
Getting support and help	A	B	C
Stage 2 Tasks			
Functioning and responsibility	A	B	C
Confronting practical reality	A	B	C
Addressing legal matters	A	B	C
Managing emotions	A	B	C
Stage 3 Tasks			
Managing lifestyle issues and practical affairs	A	B	C
Redefining relationships	A	B	C
Reconstructing personal values and beliefs	A	B	C
Concluding legal procedures	A	B	C
Stage 4 Tasks			
Constructing relationships	A	B	C
Developing new interests	A	B	C
Accepting personal responsibility	A	B	C
Accepting your new life	A	B	C

Your Point along the Road

Understanding where you are in your divorce process is important. People don't always know how they feel, or why. Sometimes people don't realize that their feelings are affecting their behavior—or they aren't even aware they're having a feeling at all. In the case of something as painful and emotional as a divorce, hidden or suppressed feelings can cloud judgment. At a time like this it's important to have clear vision. The outcome of your divorce can have a powerful impact on your life for many years to come, emotionally, financially, and practically.

Of course, many of the tasks of divorce work overlap. You can't neatly check off one task and then move on to the next. Your moods will come and go, and feelings will reemerge even after you think they're resolved. Identifying your location along this road may be emotionally difficult, especially if you're in the earliest stages of a divorce. You may find yourself feeling dismayed and overwhelmed by what's ahead. As you use your journal to explore and work through your divorce, remember to get support or help if you're finding the process especially difficult or if you simply need to take a break from your journaling.

GETTING LOCATED

You're now aware of the stages of divorce and how they typically progress. The previous journal entry has helped you identify where you are with respect to each of the divorce work tasks. Let's review the Checkpoint answers you've circled.

1. Which four tasks are the most relevant to you *now*, in your current stage of divorce work?

a. _____

b. _____

c. _____

d. _____

2. What do the tasks you picked tell you about your current divorce work?

_____

_____

_____

_____

3. What's your current divorce stage? (If it's difficult for you to easily identify the stage in your current divorce work, go directly to the next step in this entry.)

_____

_____

4. Was it difficult for you to identify your current divorce stage? If so, why?

_____

_____

_____

_____

THINGS TO THINK ABOUT

- Is the idea that there are "stages" to divorce encouraging or discouraging? Either way, why?
- Has what you've read so far been helpful, or does your divorce journey seem overwhelming?
- What kind of help do you need to get through this process? If you have help already, is it the right kind of help?

Using Your Feelings as a Guide

You now have a sense of your current stage in your emotional divorce work. But remember, there's no fast track through your divorce journey to get you from the first stage to the last. It's not enough just to fulfill your daily responsibilities and tasks along the way, and sheer will power will not be effective in helping you deal with the emotional issues. Divorce work, like any emotional work, isn't a matter of tenacity—it's a matter of the heart. *Thinking* about what you've lost is an important component of any emotional work. But the key to healing is allowing yourself to experience your feelings, and then sorting through and expressing them.

The key to healing is allowing yourself to experience your feelings, and then sorting through and expressing them.

Unfortunately, people often respond to difficult situations by allowing their emotions to guide their behaviors. This can sometimes lead to problems that, in turn, contribute to difficult emotional experiences. It can be one big vicious circle. You should be aware, then, that the goal of emotional work is not to find ways to *avoid* or *bypass* difficult and unpleasant feelings. Instead, its purpose is to find ways to *recognize* and *accept* difficult feelings and learn to tolerate, manage, and work through them.

Your feelings can serve as a "beacon" of your inside condition and can help you make sense of how to best deal with the issues that are affecting you emotionally. Unfortunately, some people can't recognize their own feelings or are only able to identify a small subset of feelings. For instance, when people experience the same emotions over and over, they may be able to understand *that* feeling—anger, sadness, or depression, for example—but they can't see beyond it. The feeling may have grown so familiar that they're unable to see that there are other emotions attached to it, layered beneath it or on the periphery. When you get angry with your ex-spouse, for example, you may not realize that you're also feeling—or *actually* feeling—betrayed, abandoned, unwanted, or afraid about the future. The trouble with getting used to *one* feeling or a small set of familiar feelings is that you may miss other feelings that are more important in helping you figure out what's going on for you.

To understand and manage intense emotions, you need to recognize, experience, and express each feeling. As you work through them, their intensity will eventually fade to the point where you can function and move on. What are you feeling *right now?* Are you confused by your feelings? Is it hard to pinpoint them? The next journal entry lists the emotions most commonly associated with divorce. This checklist can help you sort out your feelings and select the appropriate chapter in *The Healing Journey Through Divorce* to turn to in order to process your most intense emotions at the moment.

IDENTIFYING YOUR FEELINGS

Check off all the emotions that best describe what you are generally experiencing at this point in your divorce. (The numbers in parentheses next to each feeling indicate the chapters most relevant to dealing with that feeling or issue.)

__ abandonment   You feel discarded and pushed off to one side.   (4, 5, 6, 12)
This may especially be the case if your ex-spouse
seems to be moving along with his or her life just
fine or is already involved in another relationship.

__ anger	Anger often feels like a physical thing. Your muscles tense up, and you may feel like yelling at someone or hitting something. Your anger is most likely to be directed toward your ex-spouse, or you may find yourself getting angry at other people or even yourself.	(3, 9, 10, 11)
__ anxiety	Anxiety is distinct from fear and is often a generalized feeling. If you're afraid, at least you know what scares you. If you're anxious, on the other hand, you're likely to feel agitated without knowing exactly why. You may experience cold sweats, hyperactivity, or edginess.	(6, 7, 9, 10)
__ bitterness	You feel cheated by your ex-spouse, and perhaps others in your life. You may feel jealous and resentful toward others and generally victimized.	(7, 9, 11, 12)
__ concern about legal issues	You have significant concerns or questions about the legal process, your rights, what to expect from the divorce process, or how to best approach the legal and divorce issues ahead.	(3, 7)
__ concern about new relationships	You're concerned and perhaps confused about forming new relationships. Perhaps you're scared of another relationship failure, or maybe it's the *commitment* you're worried about, or the effects on your children.	(12, 13, 14)
__ concern about old relationships	You find yourself worried about what will happen to old relationships that were attached to your marriage, such as those with in-laws and shared friends.	(8, 11, 12)
__ concern about your children	Whether they're minors or adults, you're not sure how your children will respond to your separation and divorce.	(7, 8, 11)
__ concern about your relationship	There are many reasons that may require you to have a continued relationship with your ex-spouse, from	(7, 11, 12)

with your ex-spouse	custody issues to a genuine desire to maintain a relationship. You may feel unsure about what you want, how to proceed, or how to deal with your ex-spouse.	
__ depression	Depression can be a general mood of melancholy, or a full-blown experience that is all-encompassing and seems to have no end. In a major depression, your mood, appetite, sleep, memory, and ability to concentrate are seriously impaired. You may feel the impulse to do self-destructive things in an effort to find relief.	(9, 10)
__ fear	You're scared of what life will be like now. You may be fearful about your ability to cope emotionally, or you may be uncertain about practical concerns like money, raising the children, or where you'll live.	(4, 7, 8)
__ feeling overwhelmed	You simply can't cope with the barrage of emotions, thoughts, and changes facing you. You feel like running away or escaping by using alcohol or drugs. You want someone to come and rescue you, and make it all go away.	(4, 6, 9, 10)
__ helplessness	Things seem outside of your control. You may be feeling as though you're on a roller-coaster ride you can't get off. You may find yourself unable to cope with the practicalities of your everyday life and feel that you can't control or manage your feelings.	(3, 4, 9, 10)
__ hostility	Your anger and resentment toward your ex-spouse is leading to hostile feelings in which you feel as though you want to engage in battle, whether in the courtroom or elsewhere.	(7, 9, 11, 12)
__ inadequacy	You're feeling as though the divorce is your fault— that if you were a better spouse or smarter person, this would never have happened. You feel as though you're not good enough.	(5, 6, 10, 13)

___ incompleteness   Without your former spouse, you feel empty   (5, 6, 13, 14)
and unable to function as an individual, incapable
of fulfilling your own needs.

___ loneliness   You feel empty and alone, with no one to share   (4, 6, 12)
your life or your feelings. Perhaps in some way
you feel uncared for and friendless.

___ preoccupation   You can't stop thinking about your marriage.   (4, 9, 10, 13)
Perhaps you keep replaying certain scenes over and
over in your mind, agonize about what you did
wrong, or repeatedly become angry with your
ex-spouse. It's difficult to concentrate on your
everyday responsibilities or engage in a conversation
without your mind wandering.

___ sadness   Sorrow and heartbreak color everything. You feel   (4, 9, 12, 14)
the separation deeply, and it affects and pervades
all you do. It is a mood that simply won't go away.

___ shame   You may feel that this divorce is a reflection on you   (4, 5, 10)
and therefore experience a sense of personal failure,
or fear that others will see it that way. Or you may
feel a sense of shame when you tell others about
your separation or when they ask you about it.
Shame has a great deal to do with your sense of
self-esteem, but even people with the highest
sense of self-regard can feel ashamed when it
comes to divorce.

___ shock   You are bewildered and still can't believe what's   (4, 6, 7, 9)
happened. You're hoping to wake up from a bad
dream.

Of the feelings you checked off, which three are most intense right now?

1. _____

2. _____

3. _____

Beginning Your Journey

You're probably experiencing the normal process of grief and loss that follows a decision to divorce, no matter what the specific circumstances. Armed with that knowledge, it's now time for you to begin your journey through the emotional process of your divorce work.

The preceding journal entry provided a way for you to think about issues that are most pressing right now. If you want to work on any one of those feelings, or the issues connected to those feelings, immediately turn to the chapters given in the parentheses to the right of each feeling on the list above. If you want to work through *The Healing Journey Through Divorce* sequentially, you may still want to come back to this list every now and then to see which feelings are most pressing at any given time.

CHECKING IN WITH YOURSELF

Sentence starts are a good way to facilitate journal writing when you feel a little stuck. They provide a kick start to help you focus on your feelings and thoughts. They can be used as an outline tool—a way to identify the things that you want to explore further in writing.

Complete the five sentences that follow.

1. *As I complete this chapter, I feel like . . .* _____

_____

_____

2. *Right now, I'd like to . . .* _____

_____

_____

3. *Lately, I've been feeling like . . .* _____

_____

_____

4. *My most important current task is . . .* _____

_____

_____

5. *I feel like I most need to work on . . .* _____

_____

_____

THINGS TO THINK ABOUT

- Are there specific questions you need to answer before continuing with *The Healing Journey Through Divorce*?
- Do you have a clear sense of the sort of issues, feelings, and tasks that you'll be facing in your divorce work?
- Will you work your way through *The Healing Journey Through Divorce* in the sequence provided, or will you move through the book in your own order?
- Are the problems you're experiencing so severe or debilitating that you need support and help from a friend or assistance from a professional counselor?

3

Destination:

DEALING WITH

THE DECISION

MICHAEL

The day I moved out was awful, and that first night I felt like I was living in this weird sort of dream. Although we'd made the decision together to divorce, it all seemed sort of academic until that day.

I'm really not sure exactly how it first came up formally, but we both knew we were unhappy in the marriage, and eventually we decided to separate. But it was still really strange when the van pulled up to the house, and I started moving my stuff out. It was like all our problems were suddenly very real, and our marriage really was going to end. Actually, it was like our marriage really had ended.

The kids were handling it okay—they knew I wouldn't be out of their lives, but still they were just quiet and watching the whole thing. I think they knew our lives would be different from that moment on. I knew it also.

I still haven't figured out how to deal with all this. I don't feel welcome when I go back to the house to see the kids, and I haven't had a decent conversation with Kelly since we separated. But I don't think I can really take the next steps in my life until I get used to all this.

ALTHOUGH SEPARATION DOESN'T always lead to divorce if you're reading this workbook, it's likely that this separation is heading in that direction.

Your reaction to the divorce will depend largely on the circumstances surrounding the separation, whose idea it was, and how you learned of it. At one end of spectrum, if this divorce came out of the blue and was your spouse's idea, you may feel shocked, betrayed, and angry. At the other end, if the divorce was your idea, perhaps you feel sad and wonder if you are letting down your ex-spouse and family. If the decision to divorce was mutual, you may feel defeated as well as disillusioned by problems neither of you could overcome. At any point along this spectrum, you may experience a sense of failure and humiliation knowing that the world will become aware of the divorce.

The First Step

Usually, the first concrete step in a divorce involves a separation. Even though you and your spouse may continue to live under the same roof after one or both of you have decided to divorce, sooner or later one of you will be moving out, and the separation will begin.

In some instances the separation serves as a trial run to give one or both spouses some breathing room, an opportunity to establish what the problems are with the marriage and the chance to experience life without one another. Other times, separations provide a step back from the marriage that is needed to help both parties reconcile their differences. Sometimes the legal separation actually takes the place of a formal divorce and effectively serves the same role by severing the marriage.

Whatever the outcome, the separation is the first tangible step most divorcing couples experience. Overnight, you've gone from being a couple to being alone. The situation is going to vary in every case — for some, it means suddenly being a single parent;

for others, it may mean being a parent without any kids. If divorce is what you wanted, then the separation may feel like a breath of fresh air, but if divorce has been thrust on you or you were reluctant to take this route, then the separation may feel more like a chilling wind. Of course, there are those who choose divorce and for whom the separation is welcome. For the majority, however, it's not an easy step to take.

Introducing the idea of a separation is the first stage of the emotional process of divorce. Even if you initiated the divorce, you're quite likely to experience a sense of disbelief as you take this first step. If your spouse has initiated the divorce, you enter this first stage of divorce shocked. The time it takes to pass through this stage will vary from person to person, and will most likely depend on how prepared you were for the separation and your emotional makeup.

Introducing the idea of a separation is the first stage of the emotional process of divorce.

Personal Factors

Those who have difficulty confronting and negotiating the typical problems of relationships and life in general are bound to have more trouble dealing with divorce issues than those who are emotionally flexible and able to roll with the punches. These aren't judgments—these are facts. Different people feel, think, respond, and act differently. Some people react far more poorly to stress, change, and disappointment than others.

Your ability to stay in touch with yourself—to recognize, tolerate, and cope with feelings—adds to your emotional management skills, or the way you handle and act on your feelings. The issues aren't which personality style is better, and the goal of your journal writing isn't to make you a different or a "better" person; instead, the goals are to help you recognize and understand yourself better as you work through your divorce. Indeed, although you *may* change in the process of self-reflection and journaling, this is merely a by-product of your self-exploration and attention to your feelings.

Emotions and Behaviors

Although people may go through a series of fairly predictable stages in their divorce work, there's really no *one* way that people feel, react, or behave following a decision to divorce. In fact, there's a whole galaxy of feelings and behaviors that follow the breakup of a marriage. The journal entry you completed in Chapter 2 (Identifying Your Feelings) named the most common emotions experienced. Because everyone is different, there's no way to categorize the "typical," the "correct," or the "most appropriate" way to handle your feelings or behaviors after such a decision.

However, while it's not possible to identify how you *should* behave, we can say with some certainty how you *shouldn't*. For instance, punching your spouse, hurting yourself, smashing windows, spending every penny you have, getting drunk night after night, or putting the children or friends in the middle of a marital battle are not appropriate, effective, or helpful ways to express your feelings, resolve your problems, or set the tone for any future relationship you may have with your former partner. In fact, these are good examples of self-destructive actions and counterproductive behaviors that can damage and worsen the situation.

In the end, emotional management skills equal behavior regulation. Feelings quickly turn into behaviors. If you can't manage your feelings, the chances are you can't regulate your behavior. The things you say and how you say them, the way you interact with others, how you reveal your feelings to others (even if you don't mean to), the actual things you do—these are your behaviors. Because your feelings and behaviors are directly connected, the things you do reflect not only how you feel but also how you're handling those feelings.

The next journal entry provides you with the chance to take a time-out in your life and look hard at yourself and your behaviors. Some journal entries are simply records of your life; other entries give you the opportunity to express your thoughts and feelings. This journal entry will direct you to look at your feelings, behaviors, and attitudes.

Although people may go through a series of fairly predictable stages in their divorce work, there's really no one *way that people feel, react, or behave following a decision to divorce.*

HOW ARE YOU DOING?

1. What's the hardest part of your current situation?

_____

_____

_____

_____

2. In general, how are you handling things?

_____

_____

_____

_____

3. How are you treating your (ex-) spouse? Are your interactions appropriate, or are they making a difficult situation even more difficult?

_____

_____

_____

_____

4. How are you treating yourself? Are you taking care of yourself, or are you engaging in activities that you know are not in your own best interests?

_____

_____

_____

_____

5. Look hard at your behaviors. Are there things you're doing that you shouldn't be doing?

_____

_____

_____

_____

6. Look hard again. Are there things you're saying that you shouldn't be saying?

_____

_____

_____

_____

7. What are you doing that's productive—that's *helping* the situation?

_____

_____

_____

_____

8. What are you doing that's counterproductive—that's making the situation *worse*?

_____

_____

_____

_____

9. Look back at what you've just written. Are you satisfied with the way you're handling things, or are there changes you'd like to make? Explain why or why not.

_____

_____

_____

_____

THINGS TO THINK ABOUT

- Is it difficult or easy to scrutinize your behavior? What's the most difficult part about trying to "see" and judge your own behavior?
- *Can* you be objective about your own behaviors? If you were to ask others close to you what they think about the way you're handling things, what would they say? Are you able to actually ask anyone? If so, who is it? If not, why not?
- Are there significant changes you need to make in your behaviors? What are they? What else can you do to better handle your situation?

Accepting Reality

The first step to managing difficult feelings and overcoming obstacles is to face them. In these earliest days following the divorce decision, writing about the loss of your marriage will help you to confront the reality of your separation and pending divorce. Describing your feelings and the immediate issues you face can help you develop internal strength and provide a framework on which your later divorce work and important life decisions can be built. But why?

How can writing and self-expression change a thing? The answer is that they can't, but by putting your experience into words you're facing it. You're not running from it, you're not avoiding it, you're not pretending it doesn't exist. You're taking the first step in addressing any trauma by giving voice to your feelings and thoughts so you can master them. Expression helps because it relieves the buildup of internal pressure. Without having a way to vent powerful feelings, your feelings remain cooped up inside and either "leak" out or simply build up until they eventually explode. Most people who cry when sad or under unbearable pressure find that crying helps. Nothing concrete has changed, but somehow things feel better. That's one way venting can help. The expression of feelings through talking also lets some steam out. Crying and talking are cathartic and provide an outlet that allows the release of internal pressure. Expressing yourself doesn't necessarily change the situation, but it can change *you* and the way you see and feel about things.

Regardless of whether you initiated, agreed to, or were the unwilling casualty of a separation, you have feelings about this new reality. You may not have thought the whole thing through yet and may be in a frame of mind where your goal is just to get through each day without falling to pieces. How have you been dealing with this new reality? Do you even believe this is all really happening? Are you accepting your new reality or just emotionally on hold, waiting and hoping for it all to blow over?

Expression helps because it relieves the buildup of internal pressure. . . . Expressing yourself doesn't necessarily change the situation, but it can change you and the way you see and feel about things.

FACING YOUR REALITY

1. What happened? Briefly describe the immediate events leading up to the decision to divorce.

_____

_____

_____

_____

_____

2. How did you feel when you made your decision or first heard of your spouse's decision to divorce?

_____

_____

_____

_____

_____

3. What's happened since that decision?

_____

_____

_____

_____

_____

4. If you're still living together, what's this like for you? If you've separated, what's it like to be alone?

_____

_____

_____

_____

_____

5. How do you feel *now* about your current situation?

_____

_____

_____

_____

_____

6. You're either living together and waiting to separate, or you've already separated. What "mode," or state of mind, are you in emotionally? Check off the one item below that best reflects your current state of mind, or add your own description.

___ in limbo: emotionally or physically separated, but not thinking or planning beyond this

___ emotionally numb—you don't know how you're feeling

___ emotionally or physically separated and moving toward divorce

___ emotionally stuck—you don't know what you want

___ engaged in battle with your (ex-) spouse

___ secretly (or openly) waiting for reconciliation

other: _____

7. Describe your mode.

_____

_____

_____

_____

_____

8. What's this new reality like for you?

_____

_____

_____

_____

- Has this reality sunk in? Are you expecting that your divorce will move forward, or are you thinking things will either remain in "limbo" or just somehow return to the way they were? Either way, are you being realistic?
- How are you coping with this new reality? Do you need help from anyone? Who?

Shattered Assumptions

You no doubt hoped that your relationship would turn out differently than it has. More to the point, perhaps you simply *expected* that it would turn out differently. This unspoken expectation is an assumption, something you believed about the world and more or less took for granted.

The trouble with assumptions is precisely that they usually *are* unspoken and unexamined. When assumptions about the world are violated or damaged, the impact can range from eye-opening to disconcerting, disorienting, and earth-shattering. It all depends on how much you had invested in that assumption and how much of your world was built around it. Like anything else, it's not the impact that counts but what you do afterward—how you use the new knowledge that's been thrust upon you.

After a divorce, your new assumptions may be more cynical and seem more "realistic." For instance, you may believe that everyone will let you down in the end, that it's impossible to find a decent person of the opposite sex, or that it's just not worth getting too close to anyone. The shattering of formerly held assumptions can push you into deep despair and denial, or it can provide you with a deeper understanding about the world, relationships, and personal beliefs.

How has the failure of your marriage affected your assumptions? What underlying, but unexplored, beliefs did you build your marriage on? What were your assumptions about marriage, about your spouse, and about yourself? What have you learned, and how can you use this experience to avoid substituting one set of assumptions for another?

LOSS OF INNOCENCE

1. When you first married, what did you expect from your marriage?

_____

_____

_____

_____

2. What meaning was there for you in your marriage?

_____

_____

_____

_____

_____

3. What were your assumptions about your world when you married?

_____

_____

_____

_____

4. What are your assumptions *now*?

_____

_____

_____

_____

_____

Complete these sentences.

5. *I thought marriages were . . .* _____

_____

_____

6. Now, I think . . . _____

_____

_____

7. Relationships are . . . _____

_____

_____

8. The world is . . . _____

_____

_____

THINGS TO THINK ABOUT

- Have you replaced one set of assumptions with another? How can you tell the difference between "assumptions" and "facts" about the world?
- Are your new beliefs cynical and resigned, or are they open-minded and receptive to change?
- How much impact do your assumptions and beliefs have on your world and relationships? Do you think that your current beliefs will help or hinder you as you build your new life?

The Strangeness of It All

Given all the changes in your life so far, there may be times where you find yourself shaking your head and saying, "I still can't believe it." There's nothing wrong with that thought. It's completely normal and may go on for a while. At some point, you'll notice a change from "I can't believe this *is* happening" to "I can't believe this *has* happened." That will mark the point at which you've begun to fully accept the reality of your divorce and are moving on with your divorce work.

For now, it's okay for you to not simply shrug your shoulders and move on. Your first task is to take in, and cope with, the shock and disbelief of a marriage that's ended.

I STILL CAN'T BELIEVE IT

1. How has your world changed since the decision to divorce?

_____

_____

_____

_____

2. What do you especially miss?

_____

_____

_____

_____

_____

3. What's the hardest thing to accept?

_____

_____

_____

_____

_____

4. What's it like when you realize this really *has* happened?

_____

_____

_____

_____

_____

5. What makes you the saddest?

_____

_____

_____

_____

_____

6. What makes you the maddest?

_____

_____

_____

_____

_____

THINGS TO THINK ABOUT

- Does writing or talking help? If it does, in what ways? If it doesn't, are there other ways you can express yourself?
- Do you have lots of thoughts and feelings about your divorce that you haven't been able to express? If so, how are you going to discharge these feelings? Do you even want to?

4

Destination:
ADJUSTING TO LOSS

BRENDA

It's been very difficult to adjust to this divorce. I know, of course, that a divorce isn't the same as a death, but it feels like it at times. But if Jeffrey had died, I'd be able to mourn for him and I'd still have an identity—in death, he would have left me with something. Instead, my feelings now are all mixed up with loneliness, abandonment and betrayal, resentment, and fury.

After twenty years and with the kids out of the house he decided it was time for him to leave as well. It feels like I've been a wife and a mother my whole life, and now suddenly I have nothing. I don't have a career outside of the home, and now where I live doesn't feel like a home anymore. I feel like I've been cheated and robbed and have lost everything I had—including my direction in life.

LOSS IS THE basis of all grief, and it's important to allow yourself to go through a mourning period as part of a healthy grieving process. There's no clear point when people stop mourning or when their grief should come to an end. But a healthy versus unhealthy response to loss is usually measured by how well you're able to function in your daily life and, ultimately, by your ability to adjust to the loss.

Your grief is based on the loss of your marriage. People will expect you to be suffering emotionally, to be seriously set back, and to feel lost and in need of support. Your ability to stay focused and in emotional control is of great importance. Much of what happens in the later stages of your divorce will build on what happens now. The relationship you wind up having with your ex-spouse, in-laws, and shared friends; your financial and property resolutions; the child custody and support matters; and so forth all will be influenced by your reactions and behaviors during the days and weeks immediately following the decision to divorce. Consequently, an early task for you is to figure out both how to grieve and how to function.

Loss and Grief

Not every loss, though, evokes a grief response. Many losses are annoyances, inconveniences, or cause difficulties but otherwise carry no significant weight. The emotional experience of loss is limited to special situations in which the loss causes spiritual emptiness or a hole in our hearts. This emotional experience of loss has at least three components.

1. *Emotional and social (psychosocial) factors.* This aspect of loss is about its psychological effects and its impact on social relationships. How does the loss affect the way you feel about yourself (self-image), the way you think others will see you (social status), and the way you interact with others (relationships)?

2. *Practical and physical matters.* What's the "real" time impact of the loss and the tangible consequences—those things that you can see and feel in very practical terms? These are the *actual* consequences of the loss.

3. *Symbolic meaning.* Loss always involves a relationship of some kind—with people, with animals, or with belongings, jobs, and other things. Relationships always involve some kind of special meaning. They may represent a special con-

nection between two people or a sentimental value attached to a belonging. Losses, then, are also about *meaning,* and it's not unusual for a loss to strip meaning from someone's life.

As you encounter the loss of your marriage, it is normal to experience each of these aspects in one way or another.

Mourning is the period of time during which the bereaved deals with his or her loss through rituals, customs, family gatherings, or prayers. Grief, however, is neither something that you do nor a period of time through which you pass. It's the emotional experience of loss, the absence in your life.

Grief is usually seen by others as "normal" when it's both in proportion to the loss and doesn't interfere with your eventual return to your typical level of functioning. In the first case, a person is expected to substantially grieve the death of a close family member or the loss of a marriage. In most other cases, people aren't expected to enter a period of mourning because of the theft of a car, the loss of a job, or the death of a celebrity. In general, people expect the mourner to eventually resume the tasks, responsibilities, and relationships of daily life. The distinction between healthy and unhealthy grief is based largely on the ability to function despite the loss.

The distinction between healthy and unhealthy grief is based largely on the ability to function despite the loss.

The question is, what *is* it that you've lost? The obvious concrete answer is that you've lost your marriage. However, by delving deeper, you also discover you've lost what the marriage represents, the things it stands for and the things contained within it. Have you lost your partner, your lover, your best friend, your companion, or all of the above? Is it your kids, your in-laws, or other extended family? Perhaps it's financial stability or the sense of emotional security provided by the marriage. For each person, the loss may be quite different. What is it that you grieve?

This next journal entry will help you think about your loss and what it means to you. Its format allows you to work on one aspect of your loss at a time, so you may want to copy the blank format for repeated use.

THE LOSS OF . . .

1. What losses does your separation bring? Check off whatever items are applicable, and add others.

This separation has caused loss of . . .

__best friend (spouse)	__home	__self-esteem
__companionship	__identity	__sexual relationship
__contact with children	__in-law family	__shared friends
__custody of children	__innocence	__shared parenting
__direction	__meaning	__shared property
__financial support	__personal identity	__social status

other: _____   _____   _____

_____   _____   _____

_____   _____   _____

2. Pick one of these losses as the focus for this journal entry.

_____

_____

_____

3. Why have you selected this loss for your entry?

_____

_____

_____

_____

_____

4. What stands out the most for you about this loss?

_____

_____

_____

_____

5. What emotions are raised by this loss?

_____

_____

_____

6. What practical concerns are raised for you?

_____

_____

_____

7. How does this loss affect your self-image?

_____

_____

_____

_____

8. *When I think of this loss I* . . . _____

_____

_____

_____

_____

9. When it comes to this loss, what makes you

a. the maddest?_____

_____

b. the saddest? _____

_____

THINGS TO THINK ABOUT

- Does thinking about this loss in more detail help you to understand it better? Does understanding your loss better help you to figure out how to deal with it?
- Will this journal entry be useful in helping to figure out other aspects of your loss?

Adjustment and Adaptation to Change

Accommodation means making internal *changes—changes in the way you think and behave—that will allow you to appropriately respond to, cope with, and accept the reality of these* external *changes.*

As you face the loss of your marriage and move beyond the initial shock, your next task involves adjusting to the changes that the decision to divorce has brought to your life. The goal here is not to resolve all the issues—you'll discover that most can't be resolved at this point anyway. The primary goal instead is to learn to accommodate these changes, many of which are beyond your control.

What does it mean to accommodate changes? Simply, it involves accepting the inevitability of them at this time and not pretending they don't exist or will simply go away. Accommodation means making *internal* changes—changes in the way you think and behave—that will allow you to appropriately respond to, cope with, and accept the reality of these *external* changes—the changes in your environment and daily life.

One key component in adjusting to change is the need to be adaptive—the ability to flex and change yourself to meet the challenges of the world that has changed around you. By changing yourself, you can build again the sort of world you want for yourself. The goal for now is adjusting to your situation—a situation you cannot change at this time.

It's important to realize that agreeing to change doesn't mean that you want to change or that you agree with the reasons or issues that are forcing these changes. Adjustment doesn't signify agreement with your ex-spouse, nor does it imply that change is easy, emotionally or practically. Agreeing to change *does* reflect your ability to adapt to events that are outside of your control and it represents your ability to move on with your life. Use the next journal entry to consider adaptation and change in your life.

ADAPTATION

A tree that is unbending is easily broken.
The hard and strong will fall.
The soft and weak will overcome.

——LAO TSU

1. Read the poem above and keep it in mind as you proceed to the following statements in Question 2. Carefully reflect upon both statements before you check off the sentences you agree with.

2. a. *In learning to adapt, I understand that adaptation means . . .*

__I must accept the reality of the change.

__I must remain flexible to change.

__I must tolerate my feelings.

__I must accommodate the changes.

  b. *In learning to adapt, I understand that adaptation does not mean . . .*

__I agree with the basis for these changes.

__I like these changes.

__I'm emotionally okay with these changes.

__I'm not having problems coping with change.

3. What does the poem say to you?

_____

_____

_____

_____

_____

4. Write a few words about adjustment and adaptation.

_____

_____

_____

_____

- *Can* you change? What might happen if you don't?
- Are you strong and unbending or soft and flexible? Which is more important at this time in your life?

Barriers to Adjustment

How are you adjusting? What are the most difficult pieces to adjust to, and where are you having the most trouble adapting? Perhaps the issues are reflections of your personality, and you simply don't like the idea that you should have to make any changes, especially if this divorce wasn't your idea. Are your difficulties adjusting connected more to your *emotions,* or are the problems *practical*? Under any circumstances, the issues at this time aren't about whether or why to change. The current task is about *how* to change and to figure out what interferes with the ability to adapt to these inevitable changes.

The following journal entry will help you focus on barriers to adjustment. Again, this journal entry is one that can be used to think about different aspects of your adjustment, and you may want to copy it for repeated use.

ADJUSTMENT: EASIER SAID THAN DONE

1. What sort of person are you, and how does this relate to the difficulties you typically experience when faced with change and adjustment?

_____

_____

_____

_____

_____

_____

_____

2. What have been the most difficult things to adjust to? Check off each item that's applicable, and add other difficult adjustments in the space provided.

__absence of our shared friends   __living alone

__animosity with my ex-spouse   __living on only my income

__change in social status   __loss of in-law family

__feeling like a failure   __missing my best friend (spouse)

__having the house all to myself   __no daily contact with my children

__having to move   __no sexual contact

__lack of companionship   __single parenthood

other: _____   _____

_____   _____

3. What have been the three most difficult things to adjust to, and why?

a. _____

_____

b. _____

_____

c. _____

_____

4. In general, what's interfering with your ability to adjust to this new situation in your life? Again, use the checklist to help you think about issues, and add your own explanations below.

__I'm afraid to be divorced.   __I don't really want my marriage to be over.

__I'm afraid of what others will think.   __I feel like I've failed in some way.

__I don't believe my marriage is really over. __I feel that it's wrong to be divorced.

__I don't know what to do with my life if   __I'm furious with my ex-spouse.
   I'm not married.

other: _____   _____

_____   _____

5. Are difficulties to adjustment based primarily on:

__personality factors: I don't like the idea that I have to make any changes at all.

__emotional factors: The changes are emotionally overwhelming.

__practical factors: I don't have the financial or other resources required for change.

other: _____

_____

6. The three things most interfering with my ability to adjust are:

a. _____

b. _____

c. _____

7. Look back at what you've written so far. Is there a pattern or theme to what's most getting in the way of adjustment to change?

_____

_____

_____

_____

_____

8. Complete this sentence.

Some things I can do to help me get over these hurdles to adjustment are . . .

_____

_____

_____

THINGS TO THINK ABOUT

- Were you able to recognize circumstances or personal attributes that are affecting your ability to adjust? Did you learn anything surprising about yourself?
- Were you able to identify any specific ways to more effectively deal with adjustment problems?
- How important is it that you manage to accommodate these changes?

Self-Expression

It would be a mistake to think that simply discussing or writing about a problem can accomplish change in accepting and adjusting to loss. Acceptance is a state of mind, and adjustment is as much a set of behaviors as it is a mind-set. Nevertheless, the ability to express your thoughts and feelings in words allows you to give shape to them, see them, and sort through them. Often the very act of expressing a powerful feeling relieves some of its strength. Words may not be able to change the situation you're in, but they can help change *you* and the way you view the situation.

Acceptance is a state of mind, and adjustment is as much a set of behaviors as a mind-set.

One function of your divorce journal is to provide a place to get your thoughts and feelings onto paper where you can look at them, mull them over, and perhaps make decisions about where to go now. Another use is to simply record this difficult time in your life, and keep a history of what's happened and when, and how you've felt and dealt with things throughout the process. The next two journal entries provide a way to record and think about what's happened.

SINCE THE SEPARATION . . .

After taking a few moments to think about the words that best describe your reactions, feelings, or thoughts, complete these sentences.

1. *Since our separation, I . . .* _____

_____

2. *Since the separation, I haven't been able to . . .* _____

_____

3. *Since the separation, I mostly feel . . .* _____

_____

Finish these sentences by describing your current feelings in more detail.

4. *When I think of my divorce, I . . .*

_____

_____

5. Since the separation, my life has changed the most in that . . .

_____

_____

_____

6. Since the separation, I find my life to be . . .

_____

_____

_____

Create three sentence starts of your own, using the sentence starts above as examples. Focus each start on some aspect of your feelings or thoughts since the decision to divorce. Then return and finish the sentence.

1. Your sentence start: _____

Complete your thought . . . _____

_____

_____

2. Your sentence start: _____

_____

_____

3. Your sentence start: _____

_____

_____

Complete this sentence.

The most difficult thing to deal with is . . .

_____

_____

_____

_____

- Was it difficult or easy to write about your separation? What was it like to take some time to just write about life since the decision to divorce?
- Was writing a positive, negative, or neutral experience for you? Did it prompt other thoughts, feelings, or reactions? If it did, what will you do with these?

Thinking about Your Loss

In the next entry, rather than think generally about your loss, focus specifically on only one aspect of it. Because the entry will help you explore just one part of your feelings, you should make a copy of the blank entry so that you can repeat the exercise later, exploring different aspects of your loss.

YOUR LOSS

1. What three things about your loss are on your mind right now?

a. _____

b. _____

c. _____

2. Which of these three things do you want to explore in writing right now?

_____

_____

3. Why do you want to write about this part of your loss?

_____

_____

4. How does this aspect of your loss make you feel?

_____

_____

_____

_____

5. What might help you better deal with this part of your loss?

_____

_____

_____

_____

6. What can you do to better adjust to or accept this part of your loss?

_____

_____

_____

_____

One of the advantages of recording your thoughts and feelings in a journal is that it gives you a chance to review and reflect on them. Take a moment now to reread what you've just written, and then think about it. Then write down any new thoughts that you may have about your loss, or what you've written.

7. Right now, I feel . . .

_____

_____

_____

_____

_____

_____

THINGS TO THINK ABOUT

- Do you wonder if this part of your loss will always hurt, or do you expect it will pass?
- Do you usually ever stop long enough in your daily routine to actually think about your life and what's weighing on your mind at that moment? What was it like to reflect on your life in this way?
- Will you use this entry again to think about and express other aspects of your loss or any other feelings?

To Overcome Grief

To believe that you can't move on, that you can't work through this difficult time in your life, and that you require your spouse to provide direction and support is a mind-set that will keep you stuck in your grief, unable to push forward into your future.

Loss and grief are not things to "recover" from, nor are they things you should avoid through denial. There's no shortcut around loss and no way to bypass the grief that accompanies a loss. But by working through grief, you can emerge emotionally intact and perhaps stronger than you were when that journey began.

I CHOOSE TO OVERCOME GRIEF

1. Complete this thought by checking off one answer that most closely matches your feelings. Then create one or two of your own sentence starts.

My emotions feel like . . .

__the seasons coming and going because _____

_____

__a complicated puzzle because _____

_____

__physical pain because_____

_____

__a broken vase because_____

_____

__a raging river because_____

_____

Your sentence start: _____

because _____

Your sentence start: _____

because _____

2. Complete this sentence.

I choose to overcome my grief because . . .

_____

_____

_____

3. "Will's and won't's" represent your commitment to stay emotionally and physically healthy. Think about each statement below before you check off your agreement.

a. ___ I *will* stay active in my daily life.

b. ___ I *will* be patient with myself.

c. ___ I *will* connect with others.

d. ___ I *will* express my feelings.

e. ___ I *will* take care of my physical health.

f. ___ I *will* seek support if I need it.

a. ___ I *won't* expect people to know how I'm feeling if I don't tell them.

b. ___ I *won't* try to hide my feelings.

c. ___ I *won't* try to predict how long it will take to feel better.

d. ___ I *won't* isolate myself.

e. ___ I *won't* make any major decisions.

f. ___ I *won't* try to escape from my feelings.

THINGS TO THINK ABOUT

- Was it difficult to agree with the "will's and won'ts"? Are you really ready to follow their suggestions as you work your way through your divorce and accompanying sense of loss?

- Reread the "will's and won'ts" periodically to remind yourself of your commitment to stay emotionally and physically healthy.

- Are you able to accept the reality of this loss? What important thing has helped you to accept the loss? What has been the most difficult part of acceptance?

5

Destination:
RESTORING SELF-ESTEEM

SHEILA

After Alan walked out on me, my self-confidence crashed. I realized how little I knew about what he'd been thinking, and I felt like an idiot. Almost as bad, I imagined that everyone else took me for an idiot as well or else wondered how I'd failed to satisfy Alan or meet his needs.

What made it especially painful was the other woman — she was younger, prettier, and seemed more confident. At first I was really stunned because I didn't know that Alan was so dissatisfied with me and absolutely mortified because there was another woman in the picture. We'd been arguing a lot, but I had no idea he'd become involved with this other person. My whole life was really shattered, and my self-image was somewhere down at basement level.

It took me a while to realize that Alan was dissatisfied with the marriage, not me, and he had a big part to play in that. I have to admit I was pleased when things didn't work out between him and Rebecca — it just made it clearer to me that, despite the issues and difficulties with our marriage, I wasn't the problem. It took a while, but I've actually come to feel a whole lot better about myself recently — maybe better than I ever have.

While successful marriages can contribute to a sense of personal satisfaction and positive self-image, unsuccessful marriages can lead to a sense of personal failure and diminished self-esteem.

AN EARLY ISSUE in many divorces is often connected to self-image and self-esteem—how you see yourself and how you feel about yourself. No matter what your role in the decision to divorce, the failure of a marriage is often a difficult reality to accept and can have a direct bearing on both self-image and self-esteem

Some people want or need to be divorced, and for them divorce brings a sense of satisfaction and perhaps relief. The reality is that, for many different reasons, marriages aren't good for everyone. For some people, staying in a bad marriage is damaging to self-image, and leaving is good for self-esteem. But if you're on the *other* end of that divorce, it may not feel as good, and in that case you'll have many self-esteem issues to deal with.

For many people who choose to be divorced, the end of the marriage doesn't bring joy or satisfaction. Even if the marriage was a poor fit, or even destructive, and leaving was possibly the best choice, the end of the relationship may signify personal failure in one form or another. Although divorce has become quite commonplace in our society, it's still not expected. Despite the advent of prenuptial agreements and the like (where the possibility that a marriage may fail is acknowledged at the outset), the divorce is still not desired, sought after, or the anticipated end product of the marriage.

Marriages usually involve a huge investment of emotional energy. Accordingly, for most people, the failure of a marriage has a very direct impact on emotions and how the individuals in the failed marriage see themselves. While successful marriages can contribute to a sense of personal satisfaction and positive self-image, unsuccessful marriages can lead to a sense of personal failure and diminished self-esteem. In this chapter, you'll explore how your divorce is affecting, and possibly shaping, your self-image.

Self-Esteem

The goal for most people is to behave in ways that are personally fulfilling, lead to a sense of accomplishment and satisfaction, and help them feel better about themselves. That sense of well-being and its direct impact on how you see yourself in the world is generally thought of as self-esteem—a sense of self-approval or self-respect. The term *self-image* refers to the way people view themselves, and there's an active belief that positive self-image, or high self-regard, contributes to a sense of empowerment. This allows you to feel good about what you're doing and what you're *capable* of doing, and it helps you to behave productively. In turn, these positive actions contribute further to your positive self-image. When you have a positive self-image, you almost certainly have high self-esteem. Alternatively, poor self-image also affects attitude and behavior, and it feeds back into a negative self-image.

Self-Esteem and Relationships

Some of your behaviors are *direct* reactions to the world around you. You can see for yourself the direct and immediate results of what you've done, good or bad. But you also can see the results of your actions indirectly, through the reactions of other people to your behaviors.

Self-esteem is how you feel about yourself. Drop the "self" part, and you're left with *esteem,* the amount of regard afforded you by others. The way you view yourself is undoubtedly affected by the way other people see you and the esteem in which you feel you're held by them. The more important a person is to us, the more we care about how we're seen by him or her. This relationship nourishes us and is an important source of personal satisfaction, as well as a mark of accomplishment.

A successful marriage is about a successful relationship; a divorce is about an unsuccessful relationship. Important relationships that fail are often difficult to deal with because of their significant impact on self-image and self-esteem. It's normal for people's self-image to be affected by relationships, good or bad. But it's also important not to allow relationships *alone* to shape self-esteem. A bad marriage or divorce can produce lots of negative feelings and cripple self-image. Reflecting on your marriage allows you to see how the relationship affects your self-esteem. It also ensures that the decision to divorce doesn't weigh you down, bringing your self-esteem to an all-time low.

Divorce and Self-Esteem

There are many elements of a divorce that can lower self-esteem. You may feel that your marital difficulties are a direct reflection on your ability to love or be loved. People who are faced with their spouse's decision to divorce often feel unsuccessful, unloved, and perhaps unlovable. If your ex-spouse is already involved with another person, your self-image may have sunk even lower.

As the initiator of a divorce, you may feel equally unsuccessful, though from a different angle. You may feel that you've let down your spouse, your children, your family, or yourself and that you just aren't able to maintain a committed relationship. If you're leaving a bad marriage that has reduced your self-esteem, your decision to finally separate may seem like one more element of failure.

The way that you think people may see you—regardless of whether you or your spouse initiated the breakup—is also bound to have an effect on you. People feel embarrassed, humiliated, or even ashamed as they reveal to the world that their marriage has ended. If you've sought the divorce, you may feel judged by some people as unable to keep a relationship, or you may worry that some people will think you've victimized or selfishly let down your partner by making the decision to divorce. If the divorce is your spouse's idea, though, you may feel humiliated and worry that people will judge you as not good enough. If this is your second or more divorce, your feelings of failure and your concerns about public perception may run even stronger.

Occasionally a divorce turns ugly, and you or your spouse may resort to "smear" campaigns to make yourselves feel better and *look* better in the eyes of others. Here there's an actual effort to make the other partner look like the "bad" one, or the failure.

Divorces needn't turn into battles, and you don't *have* to smear or be smeared to avoid public embarrassment or shame, or to avoid your own private judgments. You don't need to feel like a failure. In fact, battles of this sort often contribute to lowering rather than raising your self-esteem. The goal is first to find ways to understand the effects of your divorce on your self-esteem and then to find ways to undo those dragging effects. You may not immediately be able to work on boosting self-esteem, but you can work on ensuring that your self-image doesn't drop further.

Use the next journal entry to think about your self-image, and how your divorce may have affected your self-esteem.

SELF-ESTEEM

1. How do you rate your self-esteem? Circle the number that best approximates your sense of self-regard, where 1 equals feeling bad about yourself and 5 equals feeling great about who you are.

I really feel bad about myself.   I really feel great about myself.

| 1 | 2 | 3 | 4 | 5 |

2. How do you see yourself in general? What is your self-image?

_____

_____

_____

_____

_____

3. What sort of impact has this divorce had on your self-esteem?

_____

_____

_____

_____

_____

4. Has the divorce damaged your self-image? How? Why?

_____

_____

_____

_____

_____

_____

_____

THINGS TO THINK ABOUT

- How much has this separation affected your self-esteem? Did you have high self-regard to begin with, or was your self-esteem low even before the decision to divorce?
- How much do your self-image and sense of self-esteem affect the way that you make decisions and live your life in general?
- Do you need to find ways to boost self-esteem or improve self-image? Is low self-esteem a current problem?

Telling Others

One of the difficulties faced by the newly divorced is informing people that your marriage is failing or that it has failed. Whether you chose divorce or it was thrust upon you by your ex-spouse, telling others is a direct route into matters you may prefer to keep private. Even if you choose to provide no details of what transpired in your marriage or the problems you encountered, the fact of separation or divorce is enough information for people to arrive at their own conclusions.

Sometimes it may sting more when you have to let people know or if they discover for themselves that the divorce was your spouse's idea, not yours. In this case, you may fear people's judgments about you—what they may assume about the sort of person you are, the sort of partner you were, and the sort of marriage you had. Saving face is one reason why people minimize the impact of a traumatic event in their lives, especially when they have a concern that others may see the event as their fault. It's easy to be less than honest when telling others about your divorce. You may leave out information that could help others better understand the reasons for the separation, or you attribute more of the problems to your ex-spouse than may be the actual case. Naming your ex-spouse as the bad guy or portraying yourself as a victim is certainly one method by which people try to save face, gather support from others, or avoid what they fear may be unflattering judgments by others.

How have you dealt with these sorts of issues? How open and honest have you been or do you want to be? How has the public nature of the divorce affected your ability to hold your head high as you walk among friends and peers in your community?

One of the difficulties faced by the newly divorced is informing people that your marriage is failing or that it has failed.

TELLING THE WORLD

1. In general, how have people found out about the divorce?

_____

_____

_____

_____

2. Who did you first directly tell about the divorce?

_____

_____

_____

_____

3. What was the experience of telling like for you?

_____

_____

_____

_____

4. How open have you been about the reasons behind the divorce?

_____

_____

_____

_____

5. No matter how open or private you've been about the divorce, what's most prompted the position you've taken?

_____

_____

_____

_____

_____

6. How do you want to be seen, or judged, by others?

_____

_____

_____

_____

7. What are your worst fears about what others might think of you now?

_____

_____

_____

8. Overall, how has the public quality of the divorce affected you?

_____

_____

_____

_____

_____

- Were there people whom it was especially difficult to tell? Why?
- Are there people you really wish didn't have to know about this?
- Have you used "face-saving" devices? If so, have you been honest with people?
- What consequences might there be if you haven't been honest or if you've placed more blame on your ex-spouse than might be fair?

Assumptions about Yourself

Self-esteem is, in part, built on a set of beliefs about yourself—good or bad. Some people picture themselves as effective, capable, and self-directed. Others may see themselves as attractive, engaging, and successful in relationships. Still others hold a less-pleasing self-image in which they may see themselves as unskilled, unlovable, or essentially flawed in some way. These beliefs are sometimes founded on actual experience, but are also usually based on a set of assumptions about yourself—the kind of person you think you are and the kind of expectations you have for yourself in life. People with a positive self-image tend to assume things will go well for them; those with low self-esteem assume the worst. Either way, social interactions and relationships, both satisfying and dissatisfying, can enhance or damage self-image and alter personal assumptions.

Social interactions and relationships, both satisfying and dissatisfying, can enhance or damage self-image and alter personal assumptions.

As difficult as it may be to imagine at this point, every adversity offers an opportunity for change. Every difficulty *forces* on you a situation that requires a solution, and every solution offers the opportunity for personal growth. For this reason, it's important to see how your divorce has affected your self-assumptions. The divorce provides an impetus for you to look closely at yourself and the beliefs you've perhaps long held and to decide what sort of person you are and what sort of person you want to be.

You can emotionally run away from the failure of an important relationship. You can vilify your ex-spouse, pretend you're not seriously affected, avoid examining your own emotions, overeat to quell your misery, drink or drug yourself into a daily stupor, or engage in any number of other ways to avoid thinking or having feelings about your divorce. You may also be replacing one set of unexamined assumptions with a new set of unexamined assumptions. For example, you may go to the gym and work out every day, go on a crash diet, get cosmetic surgery, take evening classes, or buy a new wardrobe or a car in an effort to "improve" some aspect of yourself. The assumption here is that you're just not good enough as you are and that the "new" you will be attractive to others and able to overcome all obstacles.

Alternatively, you can thoroughly examine the assumptions about yourself and those that you've built your world on and move toward an informed personal change. In the end you may decide to go to the gym, go back to school, or buy a new wardrobe of clothes anyway. But these will be informed life-improving choices rather than uninformed, knee-jerk reactions in which one set of assumptions is replaced by another.

BEYOND ASSUMPTIONS

1. Check off the assumptions you held about yourself before the decision to divorce, and add others in the space provided.

___attractive to others	___unattractive to others
___capable	___ineffective
___competent	___incompetent
___confident	___awkward
___emotionally solid	___emotionally fragile
___good enough for anyone	___not good enough
___lovable	___unlovable
___outgoing	___shy
___someone others would want to be with	___someone no one would want to be with
___successful in relationships	___failure in relationships

other: _____

_____

_____

_____

2. Do the assumptions you've picked reflect a positive or negative self-image?

_____

_____

_____

3. Check off the assumptions you held about yourself during your marriage, and add others in the space provided.

___I am a good partner to my spouse.

___I am attractive.

___I am lovable.

___I will be able to show others how good I am.

___I will be financially secure.

___I will fulfill my spouse.

___I will have a good marriage.

___I will have a new family.

___I will have a permanent marriage.

___I will nurture and take care of my children.

___My marriage will fulfill me.

___My spouse loves me.

other: _____   _____

_____   _____

_____   _____

_____   _____

_____   _____

4. What, if anything, has changed about these assumptions?

_____

_____

_____

_____

5. Keep thinking about the assumptions you held about yourself and the sort of person you are. Then complete the sentence.

Before this divorce, I assumed . . .

_____

_____

_____

_____

_____

6. How have your assumptions about yourself changed since your divorce?

_____

_____

_____

_____

_____

7. What effect have damaged or changed assumptions had on your self-image?

_____

_____

_____

_____

_____

8. What have you learned about yourself through changes in your assumptions?

_____

_____

_____

_____

_____

9. How have you changed from this experience so far?

_____

_____

_____

_____

_____

_____

THINGS TO THINK ABOUT

• Have you learned much about yourself from this journal entry? Do you think you've replaced one set of assumptions about yourself with another?
• Are you aware of assumptions that you currently hold about yourself? How can you tell if these current assumptions are correct?
• Do you think that holding assumptions sets you up for later failure? What's the alternative to assumptions?

Self-Defeating Thinking

Self-esteem is connected more to the way you see the world and your place in it than to the reality of that world. In other words, self-image and self-esteem are shadows of the way you think, *not* reflections of the way the world is (or isn't). Ultimately, we're responsible for our own self-image and self-esteem.

Sometimes our thoughts can be irrational, and we don't see things or interpret our experiences in a way that makes sense or is helpful. This is *reactive* thinking—impulsive responses to situations without much forethought or sorting through what is happening. This style of thinking and responding often hampers the development of self-esteem because it becomes part of a negative cycle in which:

Sometimes our thoughts can be irrational, and we don't see things or interpret our experiences in a way that makes sense or is helpful.

poor self-image is often built on . . .

assumptions about yourself or other people which can lead to . . .

a misinterpretation of the things that happen to you, which may trigger . . .

knee-jerk reactions and behaviors that can have . . .

unpleasant emotional or practical consequences that lead back to . . .

the sense that nothing ever goes right for you and by which . . .

low self-esteem is confirmed and on which poor self-image is built.

This is a cycle that can only be interrupted by understanding how you respond to situations and learning how to change irrational thoughts to rational and realistic thoughts.

Complete the following journal entry to explore areas in which your thinking may be irrational or slightly distorted. These thinking patterns are sometimes known as cognitive distortions.

DISTORTIONS IN THINKING

1. Briefly review each of these types of irrational thinking styles. Check off any that fit the way you think, either in general or during this particular time in your life.

___ *Emotional misreasoning.* You draw an irrational and incorrect conclusion based on the way you feel at that moment. *"I feel this way; therefore I am this way. I feel like a piece of garbage, so I must be a piece of garbage."*

___ *Overgeneralization.* You reach an incorrect conclusion that has far-reaching implications based on a single experience or a small set of experiences. You assume that your experience in one situation is a reflection of the ways things are in all situations. *"I failed to do well in this relationship, so I will fail in all relationships."*

___ *Catastrophic thinking.* You magnify the impact of negative experiences to extreme proportions. *"If I fail in this marriage, my entire life will fall to pieces."*

___ *Black-and-white thinking.* You see things as all-or-nothing situations in which things are either one way or the other. *"Either I'm a success at this marriage or I'm a total failure. If I'm not perfect, then I must be imperfect."*

___ *Shoulds and musts.* You feel you *should* do something or things *must* be a certain way. You feel that you absolutely *must* behave in a particular way or think that you *should* have a level of control over the world around you. *"I should have been more successful in my marriage." "I must succeed in this relationship."*

___ *Negative predictions/fortune telling.* You predict failure in situations yet to happen because things have gone wrong before. *"I didn't do well in this relationship, and therefore I will never do well in relationships."*

___ *Projection.* You make negative assumptions about the thoughts, intentions, or motives of another person, which are often "projections" of your own thoughts and feelings about the situation. *"She knows my marriage didn't work out. She thinks it's my fault and that I'm a loser."*

___ *Mind reading.* You feel that others *should* have known how you felt or what you wanted even though you didn't tell them. *"He ought to know that I loved him even if I didn't tell him." "She ought to know I need her support now."*

___ *Labeling.* You label yourself or someone else in a negative, often simplistic way, which shapes the way you see yourself or that other person. *"Because this relationship has failed, I'm a failure. Because my spouse wants a divorce, he's no good at all."*

___ *Personalization.* You treat a negative event as a personal reflection or confirmation of your own worthlessness. *"Because my marriage is winding up in divorce, I'm a failure—which I knew all along. Nothing ever goes right for me because I'm worthless."*

___ *Negative focus.* You focus mainly on negative events, memories, or implications while you ignore more neutral or positive information about yourself or a situation. *"It doesn't matter that I have two children who care for and love me or that I have been successful in my job. I'm no good and a failure because my marriage hasn't worked out as planned."*

___ *Cognitive avoidance.* You avoid thinking about emotionally difficult subjects because they feel overwhelming or insurmountable. *"I can't even think about it, let alone try to understand and change it."*

2. Are there other types of cognitive distortions that characterize your thinking at times? If so, what are they?

_____

_____

_____

_____

3. If you identified any types of cognitive distortions, are they typical of the way you think, or do you tend to slip into irrational thinking only under certain conditions or times in your life? Describe those instances.

_____

_____

_____

_____

4. How are cognitive distortions affecting your self-esteem and self-image?

_____

_____

_____

_____

_____

THINGS TO THINK ABOUT

- How can you tell when your thinking is distorted or irrational?
- How might distortions in your thinking affect the course of this divorce, if not corrected?
- Can you think of recent situations in which you applied cognitively distorted thinking?

Self-Affirmation

As you know by now, self-esteem is intimately connected with intimate relationships, general experiences with others, and interactions with the world around you. Self-image is also connected to and can be improved through positive self-reinforcing thought. Cognitive distortions can contribute to poor self-esteem, but self-affirmation can contribute to an improved sense of self and increase your capacity to survive difficult times.

For every disappointment and failure in your life, there's a satisfying and successful experience that can also be counted. In some cases, breaking away from or accepting the end of a difficult or destructive marriage is in itself an accomplishment. But you have to be able to *see* all the achievements and satisfying moments in your life in order to count them as a measure of your own personal success.

An affirmation is an assertion of a truth, a belief, or an ideal — a way to put out an idea and commit yourself to it. In this case, the affirmation reflects your commitment to *yourself* — your own health, goodness, strength, and ability to get through a difficult time in your life. The final journal entry in this chapter provides a means for self-affirmation.

I AM . . .

1. Name at least four things in your life of which you're proud. These can include things you've done or accomplished such as learning to play a musical instrument, special skills or abilities you've acquired, relationships you've had, challenges or adversity you've overcome, or decisions you've made. Don't overlook anything. You may even decide that your marriage itself was an achievement in its time.

a. _____

b. _____

c. _____

d. _____

e. _____

f. _____

2. Now describe at least four personal qualities about which you can feel good. These can include your generosity, the way you look, your sense of humor, your passion for issues or empathy for others, your ability to make new friends, or your attitudes and beliefs.

a. _____

b. _____

c. _____

d. _____

e. _____

f. _____

3. Complete these sentences.

a. *I know I can deal with difficult times because I . . .*

_____

_____

b. *Even though there are always things to feel badly about, I . . .*

_____

_____

c. *Although this divorce has thrown me, I . . .*

_____

_____

d. *I get strength from . . .*

_____

_____

e. *Above all I value myself because . . .*

_____

_____

f. *One thought that helps me through difficult times is . . .*

_____

_____

THINGS TO THINK ABOUT

- Was this a difficult entry for you? Were you able to describe accomplishments or personal qualities of which you're proud? If not, why not? Do you need help figuring out how to feel better about yourself?
- Do self-reinforcing thoughts help you gather internal strength or feel better about yourself during a difficult time?

6

Destination:

FINDING SUPPORT

TED

After Nancy left, I had no idea what to do. At first I felt like I ought to be able to handle this and take it in stride without turning to anyone else for help. I definitely had a "man" thing going — like I can deal with this or should be able to. But it didn't feel that way. Instead, I felt like my life was in ruins. Although there were no kids, I'd invested a lot in our marriage.

I didn't feel like I could turn to anyone. If I'd talked to people at work I imagine I would've gotten some sympathy, and the boss might have offered me some time off. But overall, I figured people would expect me to function at my usual level like nothing was wrong. That "man" thing again. I also didn't think I'd get what I needed from my family. My sister is a feminist, and I thought she'd blame me, assuming that Nancy could do no wrong. On the other hand, my brother didn't like Nancy in the first place and would probably tell me that this was no loss, that Nancy wasn't the one for me in the first place. The trouble was I didn't feel that way.

Although my friends — mostly men — offered some support, for the most part they wanted to talk about sports or thought we should go out to take my mind off things. Although I thought about talking to my few women friends, I was afraid they might think I was making a play for them by asking for their support or that they might make a play for me.

In the end, I felt like I had no one to turn to for help or support.

PEOPLE GETTING DIVORCED usually require help. But the word *help* has various meanings, and at different points along their journeys people are going to need different kinds of help.

Although most people need help at some point in the divorce process, not everyone gets the kind of help he or she needs, for various reasons. Sometimes they don't have a support system in place and there's literally no one to give help. However, for most people there's always some sort of support, even if limited. More likely, people don't know what kind of help to give or what kind is needed or wanted. Different people give different messages. Some people give off the message that they don't need help; others may signal that they're uncomfortable discussing the divorce. The result is the same: people who might have been inclined to help now shy away. In other words, getting help is a two-party process involving both support givers and support seekers.

Getting help is a two-party process involving both support givers and support seekers.

Varieties of Help

Sometimes help takes the guise of an emotional boost and/or a comforting shoulder. Other times it means getting legal advice or spiritual counseling. Help may also be a form of practical support, for example lending a hand to help out with a move or child care or providing a place to stay. It may also mean getting financial assistance from someone or getting a referral for a new job or home. In the case of divorce, help generally falls into four varieties.

1. *Emotional support.* The primary focus here is to provide companionship, nurturance, and solace. For the most part, emotional support is intended to help you feel better and to get you through this difficult period in your life.

2. *Practical support.* This sort of help offers assistance with the daily realities of your life after separation. It includes such things as financial help, help with the kids, and help getting set up in new areas of your life. Unlike emotional support, which usually comes from family and friends, practical support is given by not only friends and colleagues but also on a fee-for-service basis by financial institutions, day-care centers, and so on. Practical support refers to the sort of help you need managing your life, no matter what the *source.*

3. *Legal assistance.* Regardless of the quality of the relationship between you and your ex-spouse, if you were legally married there are going to be legal issues. These may involve adversarial court proceedings, legally binding divorce arbitration, or divorce mediation. Even without the requirement of a legal divorce, there are bound to be other legal matters for which legal help and counsel will be needed.

4. *Counseling.* This is a broad area that sometimes overlaps with legal counsel, such as mediation. Counseling covers all forms of professional and paraprofessional help designed to assist with the emotional and practical issues associated with divorce. It includes marriage and family counseling, individual counseling and therapy, and spiritual and religious counseling, as well as other forms of professional advice giving.

The help you need will vary over time, and is usually based on the type of situation you're facing at any given point.

Determinants of Help

Having said that your need for help is going to vary tremendously, it's worth understanding some of the factors that shape the kind of support you may need as well as your ability to ask for it. No single factor will determine this. Which combination of factors most applies to you?

- *Personality factors.* What sort of individual are you? What sort of help do you feel you need, and can you ask for help when needed? Do you see yourself as independent or a loner? Or do you consider yourself as someone who needs strong emotional and spiritual ties to others? Perhaps you see asking for help as a sign of weakness.

- *Gender.* There's probably little doubt that there are significant differences in the way men and women are viewed after divorce. Although these ideas are changing, in our culture men are often expected to be capable of handling whatever life hands them without too much difficulty, and without leaning on anyone else. It may be assumed that a man will function at his usual level after a separation, and men, more than women, may be reluctant to seek out support.

  Men may also face special difficulties if they've depended on their wives to take care of their home and family and the countless things that go along with those huge tasks. Under these circumstances, some men may need special help managing a household or acting as a single parent. On the other hand, although women in our society are often far more skilled at seeking out and giving support, and though they may be adept at running a household, they may be far less skilled in the broad management of single life. Women who have never worked or who have been known to others as "the wife of . . ." may face special challenges as breadwinners or with issues related to their new single identity.

- *Age and length of marriage.* People approaching middle age or older who have been married most of their adult lives are likely to face more challenges and need more help than their younger counterparts. The issues they face may clearly overlap with gender issues.

- *Practical needs.* The kind of help needed to a great degree is going to depend on practical reality. If you're divorced and suddenly become a single parent of three young children and have to take a job to support yourself, you're bound to need help.

◆ *Special needs.* One variant on practical needs involves circumstances that may, for instance, include a physical handicap or illness in which being alone presents a special problem. If one spouse had particular physical needs and the other was the primary caregiver, specialized help may be required after the separation to continue having those needs met. Similarly, if there are children with special needs in the home, the now single custodial parent may require additional help to manage the home.

◆ *Legal issues.* The amount and type of help needed here will be determined by the level of cooperation between you and your ex-spouse. A hostile and adversarial relationship will probably require more legal assistance than a mutual process in which both you and your ex-spouse have reached acceptable terms for the divorce settlement.

◆ *Financial problems.* Many people after a divorce face severe financial difficulties. These may range from not having the job skills required to make a decent living for yourself to the costs of maintaining two separate homes.

◆ *Companionship and affiliation needs.* Some people really feel the burden of loneliness after separation. In these cases, the need to be emotionally connected is paramount.

◆ *Mental health.* For some people, the emotional issues, financial strains, or other difficulties created by the divorce are too painful to deal with alone. Minor or major mental health issues can result. The strain can cause episodes of severe depression or anxiety, the development of a pattern of substance abuse, an eating disorder, or other physical problems related to mental health. Sometimes a therapist or support group can help; in other cases, a physician may be needed.

- *Varying needs.* Different stages in your divorce are going to act as additional determinants in the kind of help you might need at any given time. For example, you're likely to need more help with emotional needs immediately following your separation than months later, even though your divorce may still be in progress. Similarly, chances are you'll need increasingly less help figuring out the practical realities of your life several months into your divorce. On the other hand, you may need more legal assistance over time if your ex-spouse is being uncooperative and hostile or not helping out with financial obligations, such as child support or alimony payments.

Add all these factors up. Together they determine the kind of help needed, on a case by case basis. What's your life situation — what kind of help do you most need?

THE RIGHT HELP AT THE RIGHT TIME

1. Is the sort of support you're receiving the sort of support you need or want? Why or why not?

_____

_____

_____

_____

_____

_____

2. What kind of support do you most need? Why?

_____

_____

_____

_____

_____

3. What kind of support do you least want? Why?

_____

_____

_____

_____

_____

_____

THINGS TO THINK ABOUT

- Is there a difference between what you want and what you need?
- Try switching around Questions 2 and 3.
    What kind of support do you most *want*?
    What kind of support do you least *need*?

4. Describe your three greatest *practical* needs at this time.

a. _____

b. _____

c. _____

5. Name your three greatest *emotional* needs.

a. _____

b. _____

c. _____

6. What other needs do you have right now; what other types of support are needed?

_____

_____

_____

_____

_____

_____

7. Are the people in your support system accurately recognizing your needs? Why or why not?

_____

_____

_____

_____

_____

8. List some actions you need to take in order to get the sort of support you really want.

_____

_____

_____

_____

_____

THINGS TO THINK ABOUT

- Are your needs being recognized? If not, what's getting in the way?
- Is your need for support changing as time passes? Do you need a different kind of support now than in the days immediately following your separation?
- Are you using the support you have, or are you creating your own obstacles to getting support?

Seeking Support

By now you have a clearer sense of what type of help you need and the areas where you currently need the greatest support. Do you also have a sense of where this support can come from? Given that you have a need for different types of help, which will change over time, it's important to match your requests for help with people who can provide that type of support. Expecting certain types of help from people who simply can't provide that form of assistance is asking for disappointment and failure.

In all walks of life and all sorts of situations, people sometimes set themselves up for failure—they have expectations that can't be met, they seek attention from the wrong people, they ask for what they can't have—and are then frequently disappointed and left unsatisfied. This scenario becomes a self-fulfilling prophecy: you expect to be disappointed and are—because you're looking for the *right* things in the *wrong* places.

Getting support after a divorce is no different. To get help, you have to know where to look for it. It's not that people don't want to help, but asking the *right* people for the *wrong* kind of help—that is, help they can't provide—may make them feel inadequate and may leave you feeling alone, uncared for, or bitter. As you consider your needs, match them to the people in your support system.

You have two kinds of support systems available to you. The first is a "natural" system made up of family, friends, and others in your daily life.... You also have available to you a support system of "drafted" help.

Sources of Support

People get their support from other people who become part of a "system" of support. You have two kinds of support systems available to you. The first is a "natural" system made up of family, friends, and others in your daily life; it is a two-tiered system. This natural support group consists of an "inner" circle of close relatives, friends, and others, and an "outer" circle of neighbors, coworkers, and distant friends. You usually don't have to ask for help from your natural support system, especially those in the inner circle. As people find out about your divorce, they will naturally provide support.

In addition to this natural system, you also have available to you a support system of "drafted" help. This support system includes all types of help that must be recruited—this kind of help doesn't just pop up naturally or automatically. A natural support system doesn't have to be "activated" because it comprises people who are in your daily life, but you *do* have to go out of your way to seek out drafted support.

Drafted help includes all help you have to conscript, from legal to emotional. Lawyers are an obvious example of drafted help, but conscripted help also includes child-care centers, marital counselors, individual therapists, clergy, and divorce support groups. Sometimes there's a fee for help provided (e.g., child-care payments and attorneys' fees), but in other instances there's no cost (e.g., support groups, pastoral counseling, and women's centers). People seek out drafted support usually because their natural support system can't meet their needs. For instance, lawyers and child-care centers are usually unnecessary if you happen to have a family member or friend who's an attorney or able to provide child-care assistance. Similarly, you won't need the drafted assistance of a bank to loan you money if your best friend can lend you as much as you need whenever you need it. People in your natural support system can see your distress for themselves, and their support flows from their observations and awareness. On the other hand, drafted supporters aren't aware of your need for help until you make them aware of it. It's important to know that you have both types of support available and also how to distinguish between the two. It's of equal importance that you understand which type of support you need, and how to get it.

WHO CAN I TURN TO?

1. Whose support has been the most valuable or important to you so far? Why?

_____

_____

_____

_____

2. Describe what has been important or meaningful about this help.

_____

_____

_____

_____

3. Who has most consistently been available to you? How has he or she been able to help?

_____

_____

_____

_____

4. What kind of support do you most need at this point—natural, drafted, or both?

_____

_____

_____

_____

a. I need my natural support system now because . . .

_____

_____

b. I need a drafted support system now because . . .

_____

_____

5. Who's in your natural support system? Do you have a drafted support system yet? Use this chart to identify five people in the "inner" and "outer" circles of your natural support group and five types of support available in your drafted support system.

Natural Support Group   Drafted Support System

INNER CIRCLE   OUTER CIRCLE

1 _____   1 _____   1 _____

2 _____   2 _____   2 _____

3 _____   3 _____   3 _____

4 _____   4 _____   4 _____

5 _____   5 _____   5 _____

6. Describe how you are using this support system. Is it effective?

_____

_____

_____

_____

_____

_____

_____

7. Is your support system adequate for your current needs, or do you need to expand it? Describe how this system will meet your needs for support and help in the future as your divorce progresses.

_____

_____

_____

_____

_____

_____

_____

8. What types of drafted support might you need to add to your support network? Add other types of drafted support you may need.

___attorney   ___divorce arbitrator   ___financial advisor

___child care   ___divorce mediator   ___individual therapist

___clergy   ___divorce support group   ___marriage counselor

___counseling group   ___family therapist   ___social service agency

_____   _____   _____

_____   _____   _____

_____   _____   _____

9. Describe and analyze how your support needs will change over time.

_____

_____

_____

_____

_____

_____

THINGS TO THINK ABOUT

- Is your support system adequate? Do you use the support available to you?
- Are you comfortable asking for and getting help?
- In what ways will a support system never be enough, no matter how adequate?

Getting Support and Help

By now you've thought a lot about support and help. You may have decided that the level of support you've been getting fits your needs or that your support system isn't adequate. The goal here is for you to understand the role of support in your life and then decide what it *should* be and what it actually *is.* Once you've decided how important support is to you, and whether the support you're receiving matches your needs, you'll be in a better position to more actively seek appropriate support.

Although the words are often used interchangeably, "support" and "help" imply different types of assistance. "Help" suggests something concrete—helping with the kids, helping out financially, or helping you move, for example. Of course, the help provided *is* support, but "support" usually refers more to something more intangible—for example, offering sympathy, talking and listening, and just being there for you. As you complete this next entry, think about the difference between support and help and about how you react to both words.

GETTING SUPPORT

1. To you, what is the difference between "support" and "help"? Write down your definition of each word.

_____

_____

_____

_____

_____

_____

2. Describe the ways you can tell if you need support or help. Are there any signs? If so, what are they?

_____

_____

_____

_____

_____

3. When you need support, do you seek it out? Why or why not? Describe how you go about seeking support, or explain why you don't.

_____

_____

_____

_____

4. When offered support, do you accept it? Why or why not? How does it make you feel?

_____

_____

_____

_____

5. Name five things that interfere with your willingness to let people know you need support or help, or your ability to accept it when offered.

a. _____

b. _____

c. _____

d. _____

e. _____

6. Whose help have you accepted, and whose help haven't you accepted? Why?

_____

_____

_____

_____

_____

THINGS TO THINK ABOUT

- Do you feel you have a pretty clear sense of the kind of support you need, the kind of support you have, and how to get support?
- What have you learned about your needs? What have you learned about the role of support in your life at this time?
- Is this a journal entry to repeat again after some time has passed? In what ways do you think your needs for support and help will change over time?

Barriers to Support

Not everyone seeks out support or easily accepts it. For some, it feels like a sign of weakness to ask for or accept help, whether it be from a family member, friend, colleague, or professional.

Some people imagine that others will automatically know what kind of help is needed, and provide it. Perhaps we *ought* to be able to expect support without asking for it, but it doesn't always happen that way. Many times, people, even those in your natural support system, don't realize the pain you're in or the

People who are in a great deal of emotional turmoil, who are experiencing depression, or who have anxious moods often resist the idea of seeing a professional counselor.

practical needs you have unless you tell them. Following a divorce, especially if you did not initiate it, asking for help can be very difficult. The failure of the marriage may draw out feelings of worthlessness or inadequacy.

People who are in a great deal of emotional turmoil, who are experiencing depression, or who have anxious moods often resist the idea of seeing a professional counselor. They may feel that therapy is only for those with severe emotional problems or mental illness. They fail to see professional counseling as a means to explore, heal, and gain direction and instead view it as something that signifies their own "weakness." People similarly resist the idea of peer support groups or singles associations, because they see them as humiliating or demeaning in some way or fear that such groups are simply gathering places for people who want to meet their next partner.

Barriers to getting support are numerous. Regardless, actively seeking support is a much more effective way to get it than passively waiting for it to be offered.

BARRIERS TO SUPPORT

1. What are the chief obstructions to receiving support?

_____

_____

_____

_____

2. What sorts of resources are available in your community for drafted support?

___charitable organizations	___divorce counselors	___shelters
___child-care agencies	___divorce support groups	___singles associations
___churches and synagogues	___financial assistance	___social service agencies
___counselors and therapists	___legal aid and assistance	___women's and men's groups

___ _____ ___ _____ ___ _____

3. What are the emotional obstacles interfering with your ability to get help?

_____

_____

_____

_____

_____

4. What financial barriers are there to getting help?

_____

_____

_____

_____

_____

5. How can you overcome these emotional or financial obstructions?

_____

_____

_____

_____

_____

6. Do people recognize that you need support? Why or why not?

_____

_____

_____

_____

7. How can you let people know you need their help?

_____

_____

_____

_____

8. Returning to the first question in this entry, what are the chief obstructions to getting support?

_____

_____

_____

_____

_____

THINGS TO THINK ABOUT

- Do you get in your own way when it comes to getting support?
- Are you satisfied with the amount of support you're getting? Do you have plans to actively seek more support?
- Do you need different support than what's available to you now?

Sharing and Support

As you come to the end of this chapter, focus on sharing as another type of support. A type of comradeship, sharing can help you feel a sense of connection and belonging. Sharing can serve different purposes at different times. At this time, sharing can support and strengthen you, diminish your sense of being alone in the world, and link you with others. Sharing with others can help relieve your feelings and allow you to distribute your emotional load among others who can help carry you through this difficult time.

Sharing can support and strengthen you, diminish your sense of being alone in the world, and link you with others.

Unlike support, which you will usually only need when things are difficult, sharing is a vehicle by which you can communicate grief, joy, and everything in between. Even in the earliest days of your divorce journey, you're likely to experience moments of pleasure and warmth among other people. These are the gifts of sharing and part of the healing process.

How does sharing help? It's just one more form of expression. Unlike journaling, however, which is an *inward,* private form of self-expression, sharing is an *outward* form of self-expression involving others. Through outward contact, you help yourself rejoin your community.

But sharing requires someone to share with. Simply knowing people doesn't mean you feel comfortable sharing anything with them. There are going to be different people with whom you feel comfortable sharing different things. To share fully means being able to express and communicate all your needs and feelings, not just some of them. You may have people with whom you can share certain things, but not all. For instance, you may be willing to tell someone that you're sad and miss your loved one but find yourself unwilling to share with them the difficulties of your everyday practical reality. It's important to have a network of people or a person with whom you can share your problems.

THE FACES OF SHARING

1. Check off *all* those ways of sharing that are typical for you:

___letting people know when I need emotional help

___being with others when I need some company

___letting others know about the problems I face managing my daily tasks

___telling people about my practical worries, like financial stressors

___expressing my feelings, thoughts, and fears to others

___sharing my stories and memories

___discussing decisions and future plans

other: _____

_____

_____

2. In which three ways are you most likely to share with others?

a. _____

b. _____

c. _____

3. What are the three most difficult things to share?

a. _____

b. _____

c. _____

4. Who's in your community? With whom can you share?

_____

_____

_____

_____

_____

_____

_____

_____

_____

5. Do you share similar things with each person, or different things? What do you share and not share with each person?

_____

_____

_____

_____

_____

6. How does your community meet your needs? In what ways is your community not meeting your needs?

_____

_____

_____

_____

_____

7. What most prevents you from fully sharing your thoughts, feelings, and fears with others?

_____

_____

_____

_____

_____

THINGS TO THINK ABOUT

- Is there a pattern to the kind of sharing you do? Is there a pattern to the kind of sharing you don't do?
- What most motivates your willingness or need to share with others?
- Do you share enough? Are there things you ought to be sharing, but aren't?
- Does your community meet your needs? Do you need to think about expanding your community's ability to meet your needs? How can you do this?

7

Destination:

HANDLING THE PRACTICALITIES

TINA

I was furious when Bob walked out. I'd seen him through job problems, illnesses, and all the hard times, and I raised his children. I was hurt and shocked that this man who told me he loved me was now deciding, after twenty-four years of marriage, that he didn't want to be married to me anymore.

There was no way I was going to let him ruin my life—how did he think I was going to keep living the lifestyle he'd taught me to enjoy without him to provide support? But if he wanted a divorce, he was going to pay the price, not me. I decided to sue him for everything he had and to make sure that everyone saw him for the pig he was! My first step, and the most practical thing for me to do, was to find a good lawyer who'd help me make my life right again.

BRAD

Michelle told me she was getting a divorce because she felt like she hadn't lived her own life. We'd been together since high school, and she felt stifled and repressed by her life as a wife and mother. That was fine for her, but where did it leave me and our kids?

Maybe Michelle was right—maybe she hadn't lived her life the way she should've, but it seemed a little late to change her mind

now. But I didn't want things to get any worse between us, and I definitely didn't want the kids to suffer any more than they already were by losing their mom. So, I agreed to the divorce and became a single father. It didn't take too long to figure out what I had to do to adjust, but even so I was overwhelmed with all the everyday tasks and things that had to be done. Money was very tight, and I could only spread myself so far. Thank goodness for family and friends!

BY THE TIME you reach this chapter you've moved through the initial stage of shock, disbelief, and unreality. By now your divorce is feeling quite real. Regardless of how long it's taken you to get here, you're now clearly in the second stage of your divorce work. Doubtless, you're still very much affected by the end of your marriage, but by this time you're very clearly having to adjust to all the changes separation has brought. You're confronting and dealing with very practical affairs that range from where you live and how to pay the rent, to working on the legal issues of the divorce.

As your life settles into its new routine you'll have many issues to face, problems to solve, and decisions to make. Many of these processes are already in motion but won't fully develop for some time and can't yet be fully addressed or resolved. These include the "life" issues that are part of the third stage of your emotional divorce journey and involve how you're going to move on with your life as your divorce recedes into your past. For now, however, the issues remain quite practical and down-to-earth, involving preliminary steps in the re-formation of your life.

Getting a Divorce

You face an immediate task: deciding how to proceed with the legal details of your divorce. Some people get a divorce overnight. Some states are far more liberal than others about divorce laws, and sometimes people travel out of state for the express purpose of getting a "quickie" divorce. If you're initiating the divorce, perhaps this is something you're considering. For most people, however, this isn't how divorces proceed.

Most often divorces move slowly and are settled over a period of months or longer because there are many emotional, legal, and financial issues at stake. The way you handle the legal aspects of your divorce may well determine much of your future as an ex-spouse, and you may have a great deal riding on your attitude, behavior, and decisions during these legal proceedings. In fact, the more intertwined your lives during marriage—emotionally, financially, or as parents—the more carefully you should proceed in untangling them. Your journal can serve as a place to explore your possible courses and allow you to make reasoned decisions that involve both your intellect and your emotions.

Regardless of whether you initiated the divorce or your spouse filed first, to ensure that your best interests are served you should consult with an attorney at once, if you haven't already. If you've *mutually* agreed to a divorce, you may choose a nonadversarial legal proceeding and go through divorce mediation or arbitration instead. Even if your decision was not initially mutual, these avenues remain available to you if you both agree to them. They can only be successful, though, if you can come to terms with your spouse. These alternative ways to get a divorce are considered nonadversarial because they don't use attorneys as your advocates and champions of justice. In these cases, attorneys are used only to handle legalities and court motions, and to prepare and file paperwork.

The way you handle the legal aspects of your divorce may well determine much of your future as an ex-spouse, and you may have a great deal riding on your attitude, behavior, and decisions during these legal proceedings.

Winning and Losing

Arguments and conflicts usually wind up with winners and losers. Divorces often start in conflict, and it's not unusual for them to wind up in conflict as well. Ask yourself what it would mean to "win" in your divorce settlement and what it would mean to "lose." Remember that no two attorneys are alike. Some, following the words of former football coach Vince Lombardi, act according to the premise that "winning isn't everything; it's the only thing." An overzealous attorney may escalate your divorce from a relatively simple division of assets to a war of nerves, anger, and hostility. Remember, too, that the more time your attorney spends advocating for you, in and out of court, the higher the fee, which ultimately comes out of whatever settlement is achieved.

In modern conflict management—for instance, labor-management disputes and international peace negotiations—there's an emphasis on finding solutions in which no one loses and everyone wins. The premise is that there are no winners if any one party loses. Ask yourself exactly what it is you might "win" in a divorce settlement. Then consider what might be lost. Even if you "win"—the house, the car, the big bucks, and the plain satisfaction of coming out on top—what might be lost in the process?

If you "win"—the house, the car, the big bucks, and plain satisfaction of coming out on top—what might be lost in the process?

If you have children, what you or your spouse considers a win might be a terrible loss for them. Picture the children getting dragged through custody hearings, or imagine one of you accusing the other of neglect or abuse. Now picture an unhappy child, lacking the support of both parents as he or she moves into adolescence and beyond.

If you have shared friends, think about how a divorce might rip right through that system of relationships or tear you away from in-laws that you may have come to love as your own family. And think about how your self-esteem might be affected if you resort to "playing dirty" and mud-slinging tactics. Again, ask yourself what it means to win and lose in a divorce settlement. To accomplish the feat of having no losers, you must be able to rethink this situation and reframe it so that you can picture an outcome in which it's possible for *both* of you to come out of this whole, even if you're not entirely happy.

The next journal entry will help you think about what you want as you enter the first steps in the legal process and outcomes you hope to achieve. Your divorce is already in progress.

Accordingly, the goals here aren't to turn your divorce around. Instead, the purpose of this entry is to help you figure out how to ensure that a bad situation doesn't get worse. Try to move beyond your shock, grief, or anger. What is it that you really want from the divorce settlement? What do you need to get started in your new life? What will you require for the foreseeable future?

TO WIN WHAT?

1. What do you hope to win through this divorce proceeding?

_____

_____

_____

_____

2. What might you lose?

_____

_____

_____

3. What outcomes are most important to you? Check off all those that are important outcomes for you, and add your own in the space provided.

__children's well-being __friendship with ex-spouse __relationships with friends

__emotional health __physical health __relationships with in-laws

__financial settlement __property settlement __winning

other:_____ _____ _____

_____ _____ _____

4. Look at the outcomes you just named as important. Are they compatible? Can they all be achieved without losing something in the process? Explain why.

_____

_____

_____

_____

5. What's the most realistic successful outcome you can imagine in this divorce?

_____

_____

_____

_____

6. What's the worst outcome you can realistically picture?

_____

_____

_____

_____

7. What are some steps you can take to ensure the best possible outcome?

_____

_____

_____

_____

8. In order to work toward the best outcome, what should you avoid doing?

_____

_____

_____

_____

THINGS TO THINK ABOUT

- Is it difficult to give up the idea of winning? Would you be happy with a win-win situation?
- Will your spouse be seeking win-lose? If so, how can you best deal with that situation?

The Divorce Route

You'll face many choices along the path to divorce, including how you want to be represented in the divorce proceedings, how adversarial you want the divorce to be, and how to prepare in response to your spouse.

You may not have any choice in the way the divorce is implemented. Your spouse may not agree to anything other than a straightforward court-based adversarial divorce in which you are both represented by attorneys. However, if the choice is available, you may seek mediation or arbitration instead.

In the mediation scenario, a professional divorce mediator works with you and your spouse to make concessions, compromises, and settlements so that ideally both of you can come out of a bad situation as winners. This route requires the most cooperation and agreement. The outcomes are entirely mutual. In divorce arbitration, you both agree to turn settlement decisions over to a third party. The arbitrator, whose role is to render impartial decisions based on equitability rather than on adversarial courtroom techniques and litigation, has the legally binding power to make settlement decisions.

In the courtroom divorce, you and your spouse may choose a "no-fault" route, where the divorce is about as mutual as it can be under those circumstances. If one or both of you file charges such as adultery or abuse against the other, be prepared for a battle.

No matter which route you choose, you face many possible consequences both in terms of your shared property and your emotions. In an adversarial proceeding you can lose everything you're fighting for and may even face slander, libel, or perjury charges if you've filed charges against your ex-spouse that prove groundless or untrue. You will also have to face your own conscience and the judgment of your children if you in fact made untrue statements in anger, retribution, or an attempt to win. Though arbitration is a more cooperative process, the settlement issues are the same, and the decision-making power of the arbitrator is legally binding. If you have children, a settlement may include child custodial and visitation rights, the costs of child support and upbringing, and decision-making power over the future of your children. These decisions will affect where and how they live as well as issues concerning their educational, religious, and medical needs.

In the end, your divorce comes down to the division of all your shared property. You have a lot riding on the outcome of your divorce. Pause before making decisions, and think carefully. The previous journal entry helped you to consider the sort of outcomes you want from your divorce. The next entry will help you to think about the type of divorce you want.

WHAT KIND OF A DIVORCE?

1. What qualities do you want your attorney to possess, and what roles should he or she be able to play? Check all that meet your needs, and add others that are important to you.

__advice giver	__compassionate	__mediator	__persuasive
__aggressive	__concerned	__moderate	__responsive
__assertive	__facilitative	__negotiator	__ruthless
__charming	__go-between	__opinionated	__take charge

other: _____

_____

_____

2. Why are you seeking these qualities? What are you hoping your attorney will achieve for you?

_____

_____

_____

_____

3. If you already have a lawyer, what most prompted your choice? If you've yet to pick one, what factors will be most important? Add others that are important.

__attitude   __experience   __integrity   __record of success

__charisma   __fees/cost   __philosophy   __reputation

__courtroom skills   __humility   __recommendation   __responsiveness

other: _____   _____

_____   _____

_____   _____

4. You have a lot riding on this divorce. If you have a lawyer, is he or she the right one for you? If you don't already have an attorney, how will you know how to pick the right one?

_____

_____

_____

_____

_____

_____

5. What kind of divorce route do you want to take?

__no-fault divorce   __adversarial divorce   __arbitration   __mediation

other: _____   _____

_____   _____

_____   _____

6. Looking back at your answers, does your choice of attorney match your choice of divorce route? Do you know what kind of lawyer you want or need? Write down the key reason why you hired or will hire your lawyer, and how he or she matches your requirements.

_____

_____

_____

_____

7. Describe how the choices you've made so far in this entry match the desired outcomes you selected in your previous journal entry.

_____

_____

_____

_____

8. What are the most important issues for you in this divorce process and settlement?

_____

_____

_____

_____

_____

_____

THINGS TO THINK ABOUT

- Does your spouse want to take a different divorce route? What can you do to get your spouse to agree to the same route that you've picked?
- How can you accommodate the needs of your spouse in selecting a divorce route? What if you don't meet your spouse halfway?
- What are the most important agenda items for you in this divorce?

Managing Daily Life

Although a good part of your energy, thoughts, and feelings may be tied up in the divorce process, you still have a life to live outside the divorce. At this point in your journey, although you still have a long way to go before your life settles down, you still have to continue the daily responsibilities and tasks of your life. You have to find a way to carry on with ordinary life even during extraordinary times.

In addition to the process of making a decision about the kind of divorce and legal representation you want, practical realities need to be taken care of. They involve the "usual"—going to work, taking care of the children, walking the dog, paying the bills. Life after separation will include many practical and emotional realities that often are basic to the separation. These entail:

+ finding and moving to a new home, or adjusting to life in your existing home without your spouse
+ taking a new job or finding other ways to ensure an adequate income
+ single parenting if you have children and are the custodial parent or, if you're not, adjusting to a visitation schedule
+ developing new social activities
+ learning to spend time alone
+ running a household alone, without help

Some of these tasks may be simple for you. If you've been running a household for years, then taking care of a budget, paying bills on time, shopping, and doing laundry and other house chores are all part of your normal routine. If you're already working, continuing to earn an income won't be a problem. If you've been the primary parent, helping your kids with their homework, understanding their problems, and getting them to activities is simply life as usual.

On the other hand, if you've never run your own household, you may be feeling lost and incapable. If you're used to someone else's paying the bills, you may find that your electricity is getting cut off, the lawn is looking a little meadowlike, and your car insurance just got canceled. If your spouse took care of the maintenance and repair of your home, you may not have a clue about how to use your VCR, change the oil in your car, or fix the faucets when they leak. If you haven't held a job in years or you've never worked, you may be confronting inadequate job skills. If you depended on your spouse to parent your children, you may not have a clue about how to deal with school issues, prepare nutritious meals, and take care of your children's emotional needs and developmental issues.

But even if you have many of the practical skills needed to

In addition to the process of making a decision about the kind of divorce and legal representation you want, practical realities need to be taken care of.

manage life as usual, it doesn't mean living life alone will be a snap. For one thing, you'll still be dealing with the emotional tasks of separation. For another, you may have been able to manage many of these practical tasks before *because* your spouse was taking care of other parts of your life together. Managing tasks that were once commonplace for you now may be problematic because you have to be in two places at once: How do you both work and be at home when the kids get off the school bus? When do you find time to both mow the lawn and walk the dog? How can you pick up your mom at the airport and be home when the technician comes to fix the TV? Perhaps you're finding that one income just isn't enough to cover all the costs associated with running your life, and you need to find time for a second job and still be available to take care of the rest of your life.

What sort of issues or factors are affecting your ability to deal with your daily life? For the next journal entry, first review the list in the section Determinants of Help in Chapter 6 (pp. 75–80) to brush up on the factors that shape the support you need.

COMPLICATIONS OF DAILY LIFE

1. Check off each item on this list that's affecting your ability to manage your daily life or the practical responsibilities you have.

___*Personality factors.* Is there something about the sort of person you are and the way you deal with things that's affecting the way you're managing tasks?

___*Gender.* Is your sex affecting your ability to handle some or all of the practical tasks you're facing?

___*Age.* Is your age creating problems for you in dealing with daily tasks and practical reality?

___*Length of marriage.* Is the amount of time you were married affecting your ability to manage your life alone?

___*Practical needs.* Are the amount or types of practical tasks just too much for you to handle alone?

___*Special needs.* Do you face some extraordinary life circumstances that make it really difficult for you to handle the reality of your daily practical tasks?

___*Legal issues.* Are the legalities of your separation interfering with your ability to manage tasks, such as the costs involved, the amount of time spent in the process, or the requirement to be in meetings when you also need to be elsewhere?

___*Financial problems.* Are money matters significantly affecting your ability to manage your life?

___*Companionship and affiliation needs.* Is your ability to fulfill daily tasks being complicated by feelings of loneliness or by social isolation?

___*Mental health.* Are you facing a depression, anxiety, or other mood problem that is affecting your ability to function in your daily life? Are you developing a problem with alcohol, drugs, eating, or other behaviors that are interfering with daily tasks and life responsibilities?

___*Varying needs.* Are special difficulties dealing with practical matters somehow connected to this particular stage in your life or this point in your divorce?

other: _____

_____

_____

_____

2. In what ways are the factors you checked off affecting your ability to manage daily and practical activities?

_____

_____

_____

_____

_____

3. How independent are you? Can you support yourself emotionally, financially, practically, and in other ways?

_____

_____

_____

_____

4. Describe how it feels to deal with and be responsible for so much without help.

_____

_____

_____

_____

_____

_____

5. Where do you envision yourself in the next six months? What changes do you need to make in how you're coping? Are you moving toward building a stable life?

_____

_____

_____

_____

_____

THINGS TO THINK ABOUT

- Are you facing significant problems in dealing with daily matters? If so, what sort of help do you need to improve your capacity?
- How are problems or accomplishments in handling practical matters today going to affect tasks that you've yet to face?
- How are problems or accomplishments affecting your sense of self-image and self-esteem?

Success Builds Success

When people marry, they take on a shared responsibility for a life together. Breaking up creates a need not only to pick up your life as a single person but also learning *how* to live life as a single person once again.

Before you can deal with some of the more enduring and long-term life issues you'll be facing in the third and fourth stages of your divorce journey, you first have to develop the practical and coping skills that will at least temporarily shore up your immediate life and get you through this important phase. Your success in dealing with the tasks and issues of those future stages will build on your ability to deal with the practical issues facing you today.

Given the critical nature of managing your life and coping with practical, legal, and emotional tasks, it's important to think about how you're doing and where you may need additional help.

PRACTICAL REALITIES

1. What are the most pressing practical issues in your current life?

_____

_____

_____

_____

_____

2. Are you satisfied with how you're dealing with practical tasks? Explain why or why not.

_____

_____

_____

_____

_____

3. In what ways are you having the most difficulty dealing with practical matters?

_____

_____

_____

_____

_____

4. What adjustments must you make to better deal with practical reality?

_____

_____

_____

_____

_____

_____

5. Do you need help? Look back at your journal entries in Chapter 6. Based on what you're thinking and writing about now, do those entries accurately represent or reflect the kind of help you need or are getting?

_____

_____

_____

_____

_____

6. What sort of help is most needed?

_____

_____

_____

_____

7. What has gone right in managing your daily life?

_____

_____

_____

_____

_____

8. What has gone wrong, or been most unexpected, in managing your daily life?

_____

_____

_____

_____

_____

THINGS TO THINK ABOUT

- Are you surprised at how difficult managing daily life is, or are you relieved that it's so simple?
- Are you surprised by how well you're managing your daily life, or are you disappointed because you're having more difficulty than expected?
- Are you concerned about your ability to cope with practical matters? Who can you turn to for help?
- Should you return to the Chapter 6 journal entries on help and complete them again from a new perspective?

A Daily Record of Daily Life

People keep journals and diaries for all sorts of reasons. One use of a daily diary is to set aside some personal time each day both to chronicle your life and reflect on the events of that day. One way to think about, understand, and cope with the many overwhelming aspects of your life is to write about them.

The final journal entry in this chapter provides a format for a daily, or other periodic, journal record. You may choose to keep a journal every day for years to come, or you may keep a daily diary only during a brief period in your life. Its role is to help you "debrief" after each day or at the end of especially important or especially difficult days.

This entry also provides a place for a "thought for the day." Whether in your own words or the words of others, a daily thought can eloquently serve as a mirror for your thoughts and

One way to think about, understand, and cope with the many overwhelming aspects of your life is to write about them.

feelings or as a self-affirmation—an idea that reminds you of your worth and uplifts you. Complete each journal entry with a quotation or thought that sums up your experience of the world at that time or provides inspiration and the basis for reflection. Copy the blank entry so that you can use it again.

A DAILY DIARY

Day: _____ Date: _____

1. What were the most pressing issues on your mind today?

_____

_____

_____

_____

2. What special tasks, events, or incidents stand out?

_____

_____

_____

_____

3. Do you feel like you accomplished anything today?

_____

_____

_____

_____

4. In general, how were you affected by this day?

_____

_____

_____

_____

_____

5. What's changing over time? Are the days getting easier or harder? More hopeful or less hopeful? Are issues getting resolved or building up?

_____

_____

_____

_____

6. What's going right?

_____

_____

_____

_____

7. *Today I'm feeling* . . .

_____

_____

_____

_____

8. *I want/need to say* . . .

_____

_____

_____

_____

9. Note any other reflections on the day or this time in your life.

_____

_____

_____

_____

_____

THOUGHT FOR THE DAY

_____

_____

_____

THINGS TO THINK ABOUT

- Are there especially difficult days ahead? If so, how can you best prepare for them, and what support do you need?
- Are the days going well? What can you do to improve the chances that they'll keep improving?
- Are there things pressing for you that need your attention? What will happen if they don't get your attention?

8

Destination:

HELPING THE
CHILDREN

JENNY

I got a disturbing phone call from the school counselor yesterday, telling me that my kids had just spent an hour in her office sobbing. She told me they'd both been having trouble focusing on their schoolwork and playing with friends, and it was my oldest who said they should both go see her. Now the counselor was telling me that she wanted to see me and the kids' father together!

All I know is that the children told her they're upset by the way that Tony and I talk to each other. We've been divorced about a year, and we have little other contact outside of the kids' weekly visits with him. I admit we don't speak well to each other when we do talk, and I suppose the children hear me scold him when he brings them back late or lets them do something they're not supposed to do. They probably also overhear some of the angry phone calls from me about late support payments or how he's spending his money.

But the idea of being in the same room with him and a counselor? And what would he say? Is he going to blame me for what's happening with the kids or the way we communicate with each other, the way he always blamed me for everything? I'm feeling panicked about the whole idea, actually, and am going to ask the counselor if she just can't help the kids calm down in school or can

just meet with me alone. I don't see why she needs to see us both together.

DIVORCES—AND SOMETIMES marriages—are made especially complex by children. It's not that divorces are necessarily emotionally easier when there are no kids, but the number of complications, both emotionally and practically, are certainly increased when there are children. If you don't have children, this chapter is obviously not written for you, but you may still want to read through it, if only to understand some of the additional pressures placed on divorcing couples who have kids.

Of course, the children of a marriage can be infants, elementary school age, adolescent, or adult. And complications come with every age. To the very young child, it will be impossible to describe the divorce. For these kids, one parent or the other will simply be gone from their everyday life as they know it. For the older child, although it will be possible to explain the divorce and its meaning, it may not be possible for the child to fully grasp *why* you and your spouse have separated. The teenage child may understand the reasons for the divorce, but not accept it and start searching for parental reconciliation. Your adult children, ranging from young adulthood to their middle ages, may have reactions that include shock and disillusionment; they may not be able to accept that one or both parents now have separate lives of their own.

In other words, whether your child is an adult or minor, he or she may have significant difficulties accepting your separation. Your minor child of any age may behaviorally act out emotional responses to the separation, and young and adult children alike may feel emotionally torn between two divorced parents or feel compelled to take sides. The permutations of responses are vast, and the responses of children will vary from child to child and from situation to situation. Certainly there are going to be cases where the child supports the divorce, or even welcomes it, but even so the decision to separate and divorce is just the first step in their new lives, as well as your own. Regardless of their response, how you handle the divorce will have a direct impact on your children—on the overall quality of their lives and their emotional well-being.

Minor Children

Although complications can arise with the adult children of a divorce, the most significant problems are going to be connected to issues of child rearing. This largely affects minor children, age eighteen and under, but can also extend to young adults in college or still living at home.

In a marriage where you're still a primary caregiver to a child, your own needs may be secondary to the needs of your children. This is a difficult concept for many parents. It *doesn't* mean that you should stay in a bad marriage, but it certainly means that you should try everything possible to resolve differences with your spouse before making the decision to divorce. It also means you should think carefully about your children, their needs, your responsibility to your children, and how you can best serve as a parent after the divorce. This includes finding ways to help your ex-spouse serve as a good parent following the separation, if the children live with you.

Many young children and teenagers want to have their parents back together again. Minor children may feel a pull of loyalty to one parent or another, but they do not have the maturity or insight to understand that the problems are between their parents and are not their own fault.

Whatever the immediate feelings of the kids, they will need emotional reassurance that they are not the cause of the split and that they are still loved by both parents.

The younger or more emotionally fragile your children, the more they'll need your support. But don't overlook the fact that even mature and emotionally well-balanced children will also need you to meet their needs for safety, love, and assurance. The first things you'll have to take care of are the children's living arrangements and financial well-being. Don't leave their lives up

In a marriage where you're still a primary caregiver to a child, your own needs may be secondary to the needs of your children.

in the air until you and your ex-spouse have reached agreements on everything else that has to be decided. Instead, work these issues out soon after the separation. Regardless of how the divorce was initiated, the issues and problems belong to you and your spouse, not your children.

Adult Children

If you have adult children, they, too, may present emotional difficulties for you, although of a different kind. They may have difficulty with the idea that their parents are divorcing and even more difficulty if one parent or the other starts to date or remarries. Similarly, you may feel strange telling your adult children that you've decided to begin dating or are involved in a new and significant relationship. On a somewhat different note, you may find your adult children aligning with one of you against the other; you or your ex-spouse may even expect them to take sides. If you're experiencing any of these sorts of difficulties, discuss them with your children who are, after all, adults. With adult children, though you're free of child-rearing responsibilities and do not have to place their needs above your own, you're not entirely free of their needs and feelings, and you're not free of the emotions that their responses to your divorce will evoke in you.

THE CHILDREN

1. How have your children responded to your divorce?

_____

_____

_____

_____

_____

_____

2. Name some problems you faced telling your children about the divorce. What were you feeling when you told them or when they found out?

_____

_____

_____

_____

_____

3. What's been the most difficult part of telling your children about the divorce or discussing it with them?

_____

_____

_____

_____

_____

_____

4. What concerns do you have about how your children may respond to *future* changes in your life, such as the divorce proceedings, changed living arrangements, new romantic relationships for either yourself or your spouse, and so on?

_____

_____

_____

_____

_____

5. How has this divorce *most* affected your children, both physically and emotionally?

_____

_____

_____

_____

_____

6. How have your children's responses most affected the way *you* feel?

_____

_____

_____

_____

_____

THINGS TO THINK ABOUT

- Have you been able to clearly see your children's responses to your divorce? Have you been clearly looking? If not, why not?
- What do you need to do to ensure the best interests of your children following this decision to divorce?
- Depending on the ages of your children, do you need to put *their* interests and needs above your own?
- What do you need to do to ensure that your ex-spouse also considers the best interests of your children?

The Best Interests of the Kids

Parents, if they're not careful, can "use" their kids—no matter what their ages—to fight their battles. It's not unusual to hear people talking about how one divorced parent is using his or her child as a pawn against the other in his or her personal battle to feel good or come out on top. Here, refer back to the journal entry in Chapter 7 titled To Win What? and think about how these ideas may apply in any issues *you* may be having with respect to your children and your divorce.

Parents should definitely consider who's more able and in the best position to take care of the kids and thus become the "custodial" parent. This may be difficult for one parent or the other, especially if it means giving up being with the kids each day. For some parents, "giving up" means more than simply not being with the children. It may mean having to accept that the other parent is more "fit" or "better," or is the parent the kids love "more." This becomes a difficult emotional dilemma for the parent who gives up custodial rights. Of course, acting in the best interests of the children means acting in cooperation with your ex-spouse to determine who can best serve the children's needs at this time. It also means working together to set up appropriate and equitable shared custody and visitation rights. Even if your kids are adult children, you still may face the issue of their choosing sides or feeling compelled to stand by one parent over the other. This can be especially difficult at a time when you may be embroiled in an otherwise bitter fight.

This returns us to the idea of winning and losing. If you're already in an battle with your spouse, allowing him or her to serve as the primary custodial parent may feel as though you're giving up the kids and losing a battle. In all this arguing about who is, or should be, the primary caretaker there's a distinct danger that you're both seeing the children as property or things. They're not! It is in *your* best interest to ensure that decisions about the kids are in *their* best interests.

Acting in the best interests of the children means acting in cooperation with your ex-spouse to determine who can best serve the children's needs at this time.

IN THEIR BEST INTERESTS

1. What has been the most difficult situation for you to resolve so far regarding your children?

_____

_____

_____

_____

_____

2. In what ways have *your* best interests and needs clashed with the needs and best interests of your *children*?

_____

_____

_____

_____

3. How have you resolved these differences? Whose best interests and needs have your decisions most served? In what ways?

_____

_____

_____

_____

_____

4. If you've put your kids in the middle of a battle zone between yourself and your ex-spouse, why? What are you trying to accomplish?

_____

_____

_____

_____

5. What sort of things are in your kids' best interests—what *are* their needs?

_____

_____

_____

_____

_____

6. As you're making decisions, what's the most difficult part of ensuring that you're fully considering the needs and best interests of your children?

_____

_____

_____

_____

_____

Kids Have Problems Too

Perhaps one of the most difficult and enduring things to handle is the fact that your kids may suffer emotionally as a result of your divorce. Most parents want to avoid the development of emotional problems in their kids, but don't necessarily know how.

The problems that kids may face during and following a divorce are too numerous to list fully, and the subject is beyond the scope of this workbook. Issues will be compounded not only by the actual events of the divorce and the behaviors of both parents, but also by the age of the child and developmental issues. A toddler or an elementary school age child will face an entirely different set of circumstances than an adolescent, for instance. An adult child will deal with adjustment difficulties that have little to do with personal development or self-esteem, but may nevertheless face other significant problems and issues stemming from your divorce. Kids under age eighteen may develop major self-esteem issues if they feel that they are somehow responsible for the divorce. Children from toddlers to adolescents may feel that they somehow have been the cause of the rift between their parents.

Asking a child to choose one parent over another is an additional problem. The choices here aren't just about with whom the child wants to live, but also which parent the child will fraternize with and love *after* custody issues are resolved. Some parents have a difficult time knowing that their kids love their ex-spouse as well, especially if they hold the other parent to blame in some way, feel their ex-spouse is not acting fairly or responsibly after the divorce, or just feel they got the short end of the stick.

Another parental behavior that can lead to problems in a child involves the use of the children as "spies" to find out what the other parent is doing, thinking, and feeling. This isn't the same as simply asking "How's your father doing?" or "What's happening with your mom's job?" The questions in this scenario are far more personal and allow one parent to learn about the other, without directly taking the responsibility of doing so themself. For whatever direct or indirect reasons it may serve you, asking your children to be your informants does not serve them or their mental health.

Having kids act as mediators or message carriers will cause major problems for them.

In a similar vein, having kids act as mediators or message carriers will cause major problems for them. Sometimes the messages are benign and are intended solely to relay information from one parent to another—an invitation to a family event, for instance, or a notice to attend a school meeting. Other times, the message may be angry or malicious—for example, having your son tell his mother that she can't see him that weekend or telling your daughter to instruct her father that he can't have his girlfriend come over while she is visiting. This sort of parental behavior incorrectly assumes that the children feel okay about delivering messages, but in fact this presents an enormous task for a child while allowing the parents to remove themselves from the responsibility of direct communication. Children may come to dread visiting one parent or returning from a visit because of the messages they have to carry. The child may feel pushed into simply choosing not to visit a parent or feeling guilty for the messages being delivered. This in turn can create self-esteem, emotional, and other developmental problems for the child.

Your kids are often smarter than you think. Even if you're not directly asking them to snoop and report on their other parent or requiring them to pass messages and deliver information between you, they'll know what's happening. But although they may be smarter than you think, they're not as emotionally well developed as you might want them to be. Consequently, they're not likely to tell you to stop asking them about their other parent, or stop giving them messages to deliver to the other parent despite their discomfort with the situation. Instead, they'll feel forced to continue being a "mole" for you.

Sometimes parents confide in their children, telling them things about themselves or their feelings or sharing with them information about their other parent that just isn't appropriate. Sometimes age is the determining factor of what is and isn't appropriate; at other times the subject matter itself determines the line you should draw. It may be okay to share your feelings with your thirty-year-old daughter, but it isn't necessarily appropriate to share those same feelings with your twelve-year-old son. Telling your child that your ex-spouse is no good may damage that child's relationship with the other parent, or with you, and sharing with your children how lonely you feel or how low your self-esteem has sunk may leave your kids feeling overwhelmed and anxious. Sharing with your adult child the intimate details of your sex life *may* be okay (it also may never be okay, depending on the kind of relationship you have), but it's definitely not appropriate to share this sort of information with your teenage child. Sex education is one thing; telling your teenager about your sex life is something quite different.

There are many problems that your children may face during and after your divorce. These range from missing one parent or the other or simply missing the security of the intact family to the development of serious insecurity and trust issues. Another issue to be aware of is the "parentification" of children. This can happen when the child of a divorce is expected to take over some or all of the responsibilities of the parent who's left, which range from household chores to providing child care for younger siblings. Sometimes, parentification can include becoming a companion to one parent or the other. It's important not to use your adolescent child, for instance, as your escort to a social function or as a cohost or hostess when you entertain. Even if your chil-

In all the problems you'll face as a divorced parent with children, you'll need to figure out where to draw the line and decide how to best take care of yourself and the emotional welfare of your kids.

dren are young adults or older, don't expect them to become your close friend or social partner.

In all the problems you'll face as a divorced parent with children, you'll need to figure out where to draw the line and decide how best to take care of yourself and the emotional welfare of your kids. Of course, kids sometimes have to work their way through their problems for themselves. The real trick for you, though, is to ensure that your problems don't become the basis of your children's problems.

When it comes to your kids, consider this synopsis of do's and dont's.

Do

- make sure that they don't feel they have to take sides.
- make sure they get to spend good time with both their parents.
- resolve problems with your ex-spouse without involving them.
- ensure that they feel loved and cared for.
- ensure that their financial needs are met.
- keep any blame for the divorce between you and your ex-spouse.
- ensure that their lives don't change in radical ways because of your divorce.
- help them understand that you're responsible for your own well-being.
- encourage them to live their own lives and have their own friends.

Don't

- make them choose between parents.
- make them feel as though they have only one parent.
- put them between you and your ex-spouse, or in the middle of divorce wars.
- deprive them of emotional support.

- deprive them of financial support.
- blame them for what went wrong.
- force them to radically change their lifestyle.
- make them responsible for your emotional well-being.
- let your divorce interfere with their social life and peer relationships.

"SEEING" YOUR KIDS

1. In what ways have your children adjusted to your divorce? Have you noticed any significant changes in their emotions or behaviors?

_____

_____

_____

_____

_____

2. List some concerns you have about the way that any of your children have adjusted or changes in their mood or behavior. Name both the positive and negative aspects.

_____

_____

_____

_____

_____

3. Put yourself in your children's shoes, and describe what you think your kids are going through.

_____

_____

_____

_____

_____

4. What do your children most need from you to adjust to this divorce in the best possible way?

_____

_____

_____

_____

5. What do the kids most need from you and your ex-spouse for their best possible personal adjustment?

_____

_____

_____

_____

6. Are you putting too much responsibility on your children in certain areas? If so, in what ways?

_____

_____

_____

_____

7. In what ways is your divorce affecting the lives of your children?

_____

_____

_____

_____

8. What changes must you personally make to most effectively help your kids?

_____

_____

_____

_____

- Are you able to spot problems your kids may be having? Do you need to find better ways to see what's happening emotionally for your children?
- Are you worried about your kids? If so, how can you help them or where can you seek outside help?
- Do you need to talk to your kids more? Do you need to find out more about how they're feeling and what they need?
- Are you asking or expecting your kids to fill needs in your life that they shouldn't be filling at their age, or at all?

Helping Your Child

The behavior of your children, as well as their mood, is often an obvious indicator of how they're feeling. Unusual moods or clear changes in behaviors that develop during and after the separation are often mirrors of what's going on "inside" your child and may be a reflection that things are not all right.

Learning to understand your kids, and what you can do to help them, is not necessarily a simple task. Talking to friends and neighbors who themselves have been divorced and have raised kids is a good place to get started. There are also many self-help books on parenting and child rearing available in libraries and bookstores. Discussing your children with a trained school counselor or with your own therapist is an excellent way to figure out how to best deal with your kids and help them through this difficult time in their lives. Talking to a school counselor or teacher who knows and works with your kids has special value, because they can see problems that may be developing in the school environment, including problems with concentration and attention, mood, peer interactions, and other behaviors. You can also join a parents' support group, many of which are run in communities on a regular basis.

Learning to understand your kids, and what you can do to help them, is not necessarily a simple task.

There are also available sources of help for your kids. Some schools run support or discussion groups for children going through divorce, and such groups may also be available through local community centers, mental health clinics, and counseling centers. Depending on your child's age, you may also want to consider individual counseling to help him or her figure out how to deal with personal issues, the stressors of life after divorce, and just plain growing up in a complex world.

Talking to your kids is a great way to understand them but only if you've built a trusting, open, and communicative relationship. If it's difficult to talk openly with your kids, or the issues have become very painful and awkward, consider family counseling. This can be a great resource to help you better understand your kids and have them understand you, learn how to communicate, and create new ways to handle difficult situations.

However, the best help you can give your children is to see them as *people* and to consider *their* needs and *their* best interests. Seek ways to assure them—not just through the things you say but also through your own behaviors and the decisions you make—that their lives will not be ruined through your divorce.

The best help you can give your children is to see them as people *and to consider* their *needs and* their *best interests.*

Blended Families

Sometimes, your kids aren't the children of your most recent ex-spouse or vice versa. You may have children from a previous relationship for whom your spouse was a stepparent. Or either one of you may have kids from prior relationships *and* children from this marriage. These families are often called blended families, but the difficulties for the kids are just about the same as with any divorce.

The sense of security for your kids may have already been challenged by a previous divorce. They may have come into this blended family with some emotional insecurities and misgivings, and another separation is not going to help their sense of stability, security, permanence, and sometimes confidence in their parents. But overall the issues are the same. How can you best help your kids, whether they're your own, your step-, or your "shared" kids? How can you ensure that you and your ex-spouse keep the children's best interests central to any decisions you make regarding the separation arrangements? How can you both ensure that your children maintain their self-esteem and trust and feel supported by the most important adults in their lives?

Sharing Responsibility

On a final note, being a good parent means taking full responsibility for your children, even if you're not the primary custodial parent after the divorce. Sharing decisions about your shared child's future and allowing for religious, racial, or cultural differences between you and your ex-spouse will be important in helping your children to feel unfettered in their love and affection for you both. How you deal with parental visitations; holidays and family gatherings on both sides of the family; and special occasions like graduations, bar mitzvahs and bas mitzvahs, confirmations, and weddings will be very important in how well you serve as a parent and mentor to your child.

In the final journal entry of this chapter, you'll have the chance to think about the aftermath of custody decisions. This is a format you may wish to use repeatedly, so consider making a copy of it before you begin.

AFTER THE DIVORCE

1. If you've become the custodial parent, what's life been like as a single parent? If you're the noncustodial parent, what's it been like to lose daily contact with the children?

_____

_____

_____

_____

_____

_____

2. Whether you're the primary custodial parent or not, a decision was made to place one of you in that role. Either way, how did that decision make you feel? Did you feel gratified by the decision or were you hurt, and if so, why?

_____

_____

_____

_____

_____

_____

3. If there was/is a fight for custody, or your kids were/are involved in such a fight, how have they been affected by the process?

_____

_____

_____

_____

_____

4. How can you best help your kids recover from or deal with fights over custody issues?

_____

_____

_____

_____

5. Are your kids now suffering in some way because of custody issues or because of changes in the parenting situation? How are they being affected?

_____

_____

_____

_____

_____

6. What are the greatest obstacles to cooperation between you and your ex-spouse when it comes to the kids?

_____

_____

_____

_____

_____

_____

7. How can you best resolve differences with your ex-spouse when it comes to decisions about your kids?

_____

_____

_____

_____

_____

_____

8. What are your three greatest priorities as a parent?

a. _____

b. _____

c. _____

9. Pick one of your priorities and write about it.

_____

_____

_____

_____

_____

_____

9

Destination:
DEALING WITH
EMOTIONS

RONNIE

I was so angry after Joey left that I thought I could strangle some-one, and I was so hurt that it felt like I could cry myself to death. I didn't even know if I still wanted to live. Life without my husband seemed completely bare, and I kept asking myself what good is liv-ing without the man I'd been with since I was sixteen.

As though that wasn't bad enough, Joe left me for a woman who just oozed sex and was half my age. I felt like I couldn't face other people and figured they'd be laughing at me or feeling sorry for me because I couldn't see what he'd been doing for at least two years before I discovered his affair. I was so hurt. And I didn't know how to tell the kids about what kind of man their father was.

I was so full of emotions that I didn't know how I felt. One minute I was angry, and the next I was crying. I felt scared, hurt, resentful, mad as hell, and jealous all at once. I felt like I was going to burst, and I was afraid I would.

THERE'S NOTHING QUITE as basic as feelings. Whether you want them or not, there they are. In fact, many people don't want feel-ings, or at least not the bad ones. They do everything they can to block out the "bad" feelings and pursue the "good" ones. In some cases, this leads to emotional numbness and denial, impetuous pleasure seeking, substance abuse, and other inappropriate responses to difficult feelings.

At the outset of the separation and divorce process, negative feelings like anger, shame, and embarrassment; betrayal and rejection; and hopelessness are bound to show up for most people. If you were unprepared for your spouse's decision to divorce, you're almost certainly going to experience feelings of this sort. Within a matter of days or a few weeks, as the long-term effects of this decision become apparent, you may experience depression, anxiety, and helplessness and perhaps an overwhelming grief for the love and marriage now lost.

At the outset of the separation and divorce process, negative feelings like anger, shame, and embarrassment; betrayal and rejection; and hopelessness are bound to show up.

Feelings usually come before thought—your first reaction to a situation. You've no doubt been flooded with feelings since the decision to divorce, most likely without any conscious thought. But now you know that expressing feelings doesn't exorcize them. No matter how much you talk or write about your feelings, they simply don't just vanish. Nevertheless, expressing feelings does help you to vent them, thus relieving their pressure, and helps you, too, to understand, tolerate, and manage them so that they don't boil over and erupt into behaviors that you may later (or even immediately) regret.

Dealing with Feelings

Some of your feelings are going to pass only with time, no matter what you do. Other feelings may signal the need for some sort of action. For instance, you may be angry at your ex-spouse because you feel let down and abandoned, or you may feel sad at the end of your marriage. In these cases, there may not be much you can do about your feelings other than accept, endure, and manage them. But feelings of worry or helplessness may tell you to take some action. Solving a legal issue associated with the divorce, getting concrete support from family or friends, ensuring a new source of income, or building new relationships may alleviate some types of feelings.

In other words, some feelings are related to personal psychology and spiritual issues—self-esteem and personal worth, a sense of belonging and connection, or the experience of being loved and cared for—whereas other feelings are more likely to be connected to practical or lifestyle issues—the loss of income or home, issues of single parenthood, or fears of being left alone. In the latter case, your feelings may go away once you've resolved the practical matters. But feelings connected to your sense of who you are and your reactions to relationships, expectations, and change will have to be accepted and tolerated—just as you learned to accept the life issues that have resulted in these feelings. Your emotions won't pass simply because you've resolved practical issues. In fact, they may linger long after you've worked out the divorce settlement and have settled into your new life. Divorced couples often harbor bad feelings for one another years after their divorce.

Dealing with your feelings means understanding, tolerating, and managing them. It doesn't mean punching, eating, spending, drinking, or drugging them away. Being able to distinguish the basis for feelings can also help you recognize that there are some things you can change and some things you can't—a sentiment that has been captured in a poem famous for inspiring people to overcome adversity of every kind:

Being able to distinguish the basis for feelings can also help you recognize that there are some things you can change and some things you can't.

> *Grant me the serenity to accept the things I cannot change,*
> *courage to change the things I can,*
> *and wisdom to know the difference.*
> —REINHOLD NIEBUHR

Some feelings are attached to a sense of personal loss (psychological or spiritual needs); others are directed at practical needs (e.g., how to live and manage your life). The next journal entry will help you to think about and distinguish between these types of feelings. As this entry focuses on only one feeling at a time, you should copy it so that you can use it again to sort through other feelings.

THE BASIS OF YOUR FEELINGS

1. What are some of the negative feelings that you've experienced since the initial decision to divorce? Use the checklist to help think about your emotions, and add others to the bottom of the list. Next to each emotion you check, identify whether this feeling is psychological or spiritual in basis or more connected to your practical needs. Then write a few words about each feeling you've checked.

	Psychological/Spiritual		Practical
__abandoned	__	__	_____
__afraid	__	__	_____
__angry	__	__	_____
__anxious	__	__	_____
__ashamed	__	__	_____
__betrayed	__	__	_____
__bitter	__	__	_____
__detached	__	__	_____
__disappointed	__	__	_____
__foolish	__	__	_____
__guilty	__	__	_____
__helpless	__	__	_____
__hopeless	__	__	_____
__hurt	__	__	_____
__ignored	__	__	_____
__incapable	__	__	_____
__irritated	__	__	_____
__lonely	__	__	_____
__numb	__	__	_____
__overwhelmed	__	__	_____
__regretful	__	__	_____
__rejected	__	__	_____

__remorseful   __   __   _____

__sad   __   __   _____

__shocked   __   __   _____

__sorrowful   __   __   _____

__trapped   __   __   _____

__vulnerable   __   __   _____

__worried   __   __   _____

__worthless   __   __   _____

__yearning   __   __   _____

_____

_____

_____

_____

2. Which five psychological and which five practical emotions have been the most persistent?

Psychological/Spiritual	Practical
a. _____	_____
b. _____	_____
c. _____	_____
d. _____	_____
e. _____	_____

3. Pick any *one* of these emotions to work on for the remainder of the entry.

_____

4. Why have you picked this emotion for your entry?

_____

_____

_____

_____

5. What is it about this emotion that makes it more psychological/spiritual rather than practical in nature?

_____

_____

_____

_____

_____

6. What most triggers this feeling for you? Are there certain times, events, or thoughts that tend to "activate" this emotion?

_____

_____

_____

_____

_____

7. Is there something you can do to alleviate or reduce the intensity of this particular emotion?

_____

_____

_____

_____

_____

_____

8. How have you been coping with this feeling?

_____

_____

_____

_____

_____

_____

Recognizing Feelings

Since your separation you've probably been trying to manage, and hoping to eventually overcome, unpleasant feelings. But in most cases, in order to manage a feeling you first have to know you're having one. To prevent yourself from being overwhelmed by a particularly strong feeling, you must be able to understand it. This ability to correctly recognize and interpret your feelings as you have them is called *interoceptive* awareness, or the ability to know *how* you feel. People with poor interoceptive awareness often misidentify their feelings.

Alternatively, *introspective* awareness is understanding *why* you feel the way you do—the ability to look inside and focus on your own thoughts and feelings. Taking the time to think about your feelings and reflect on your thoughts is one way to better know yourself and to adjust to the world around you. It's also an important technique that allows people to stop their feelings from immediately being acted out as behaviors. Recognizing that you have a feeling becomes the buffer between emotion, thought, and behavior.

In spontaneous behavior, emotions tend to turn immediately into actions—you feel something, then you act on it. Generally there's nothing wrong with acting spontaneously. Indeed, life would be odd and rather artificial if we had to think about every

This ability to correctly recognize and interpret your feelings as you have them is called interoceptive *awareness, or the ability to know* how *you feel.*

feeling we had before we expressed it, and about the consequences of every behavior before we acted. However, there are also times when it's imperative to think before you act. It's this awareness that leads to socially and personally responsible behavior. Sometimes acting on an angry feeling is the right thing to do; other times, such behavior may be disastrous. The ability to regulate spontaneity and contemplation is key to a balanced life.

This process of recognizing and thinking about your feelings is a step toward emotional regulation.

Crying is a good example of spontaneous behavior that is a great emotional outlet. But yelling at someone, overeating, and consuming too much alcohol are all examples of acting out an emotion in a way that may be destructive to your relationships and yourself. At this time in your life, you need to be aware of your feelings and how they're affecting you and to be conscious of the consequences of your behaviors.

This process of recognizing and thinking about your feelings is a step toward emotional *regulation*. Regulation doesn't mean preventing your feelings; rather, it allows you to find ways to express them positively instead of acting them out inappropriately. Simply put, coping with your feelings doesn't mean you don't have them. But it does mean you don't let them overwhelm you. Something as simple as stopping and thinking about how you're feeling at a difficult moment can be a very useful way to regulate and cope with that emotion. By linking your feelings to your thoughts, you also link your feelings to your behaviors. You stop acting impulsively or reactively. You begin to see yourself more clearly; in turn, you're better able to see *how* to respond and what actions to take.

The next journal entry will help you recognize how you're feeling, and why. It provides a checklist of very basic feelings, many of which you'll experience during your divorce journey. This is a journal entry you may want to repeat as you learn to focus on and process your emotions. Photocopy this entry format so that you may use it again. Complete this journal entry shortly before or after a situation that may be emotional for you or when you find feelings washing over you. It's a simple way to help pick up and understand a feeling.

MY FEELINGS

How I Feel   *Why I Feel This Way*

___abandoned   _____

___afraid   _____

___amused   _____

___angry   _____

___anxious   _____

___ashamed   _____

___betrayed   _____

___bitter   _____

___detached   _____

___disappointed   _____

___foolish   _____

___guilty   _____

___happy   _____

___helpless   _____

___hopeful   _____

___hopeless   _____

___hurt   _____

___ignored   _____

___incapable   _____

___irritated   _____

___lonely   _____

___numb   _____

___overwhelmed   _____

___regretful   _____

___remorseful   _____

___sad   _____

___shocked   _____

___sorrowful   _____

___trapped   _____

___vulnerable _____

___worried   _____

___worthless   _____

___yearning   _____

THINGS TO THINK ABOUT

- Were you easily able to pick out feelings? If you've used this journal format more than once, is it getting easier to recognize your feelings?
- Do you understand why you feel the way you do? Is it important to understand how you feel?
- Do you want to be able to regulate your feelings? Does understanding your feelings help you to regulate them?

Coping with Feelings

Recognizing feelings is an important skill to develop. Even as you recognize and identify your feelings, though, you still may not know how to deal with them. What do you do with these feelings that you've now identified? How do you tolerate them?

Anger is often a very tangible feeling. Sometimes it pushes people into saying inappropriate things, and sometimes anger is so intense that it leads to violence. You may feel that the only way you can resolve and rid yourself of your angry feelings is through revenge or some other act of retribution.

Violent behaviors never help a situation. In fact, they are likely to make the situation far worse and may even land you in serious legal trouble. If you find yourself thinking that nothing short of violence or other forms of aggression will relieve your anger or other negative emotions, you should seek professional help. Similarly, if throwing dishes and punching holes in the wall is the only way you can relieve yourself of feelings, consider speaking to your primary care physician, clergy member, or a professional counselor. Not only are you hurting yourself and damaging your own property, you're doing it in vain; you aren't solving any of your problems. If your anger must be vented physically, consider playing a sport or hitting a punching bag or making a yeast bread to work out your anger as you knead the dough.

Pain manifests itself differently from anger and often lasts longer. The pain from a failed marriage feels just as real as the pain from a physical injury—but here the blow is to your psyche, your heart, or your ego. As with any pain, it *hurts*. When people hurt, they sometimes decide that hurting someone else will make them feel better, but, of course, it doesn't. It just makes the situation much worse.

Loneliness is another very difficult feeling to adjust to. Whether your marriage lasted one year or fifty, it can be a shock to suddenly spend your days, evenings, weekends, or vacations alone. Some people allow the despair of being alone to wash over them without taking any steps toward rebuilding a social life. But allowing loneliness to take over your life can be one step along the route to a full-blown depression. Finding ways to appreciate being alone at times and using that solitude *productively* is one way to handle suddenly being single.

Of course, there are myriad other feelings that are difficult to cope with. The issues aren't about *whether* you'll have feelings but about *how* you'll deal with them. Your next journal entry will focus you on ways to cope. It will also help you to think about behaviors to avoid when you are experiencing difficult emotions. Copy the entry before completing it so that you can use it to explore other emotions at a later time.

The pain from a failed marriage feels just as real as the pain from a physical injury—but here the blow is to your psyche, your heart, or your ego. As with any pain, it hurts.

RESPONDING TO FEELINGS

1. Look back at the checklist you completed in the first journal entry in this chapter (pp. 138–140). Which five emotions are the most difficult for you to manage?

a. _____

b. _____

c. _____

d. _____

e. _____

2. Pick one of these emotions to explore in depth in this entry.

_____

_____

3. Describe your feeling in words.

_____

_____

_____

_____

_____

4. Why is this feeling so difficult to handle?

_____

_____

_____

_____

_____

5. How do you feel like behaving when you have this feeling?

_____

_____

_____

_____

6. What should you *not* do when you're feeling this way? Why?

_____

_____

_____

_____

_____

7. If the way you behave in response to this feeling is inappropriate, what are the possible consequences you might face?

_____

_____

_____

_____

8. What are five ways you might be able to deal with this feeling? Use this checklist and add your own ideas.

___cry   ___hit a punching bag   ___talk to a counselor

___do something physical   ___make or build something ___talk to a friend

___do something social   ___play a sport   ___talk to a minister

___draw   ___read a book   ___write

___go running   ___take a walk   ___yell into a pillow

other: _____ _____ _____

       _____ _____ _____

       _____ _____ _____

       _____ _____ _____

9. What stressor or event in your life right now most contributes to the difficulties you experience with this emotion?

_____

_____

_____

_____

- You've identified ways to cope and behaviors to avoid when you have this feeling. What will stop you from using effective coping strategies? How can you prevent yourself from behaving inappropriately?
- What stops you from turning to friends or others for assistance and support when you feel lousy? Are there people you *can* turn to? Do you need to get more help into your life?
- If you need more help in coping, how and where will you find it?

Staying in Touch with Yourself

Some feelings last awhile and are more like a collection of feelings than a single emotion. These are *moods*—a set of underlying feelings that color everything for you while you are in that mood.

There are good moods and bad ones—happy, angry, satisfied, depressed. Moods are only thought of as problems when they frequently fluctuate, from high to low or when the most common mood is a bad mood of some kind. When moods are pervasive over time, they sometimes begin to interfere with your ability to function. At that point, a mood may be developing into a disorder that requires treatment. For instance, if you're often depressed and you find that *everything* is affected by your mood— your sleep, your appetite, your energy, your ability to concentrate—this may be a problem. The same is true if you're anxious all the time, or angry. Moods can become so deep that they change the way you see and feel about everything.

The most useful time to write about a feeling is when you're having it. Similarly, the most useful time to think about a mood is when you're in it. *Complete the next journal entry only when you're in the grip of a mood.* Look the entry over now, but skip it and return only when you can write about a mood that you're actually experiencing. You may not *want* to write when in an emotionally difficult mood, but this challenge will be helpful in your recovery.

If you repeat the entry each time you're caught in the same or different mood, you'll learn a great deal about yourself. Like

If you're often depressed and you find that everything *is affected by your mood—your sleep, your appetite, your energy, your ability to concentrate—this may be a problem.*

most of the journal entries in *The Healing Journey Through Divorce*, this entry can be repeated. Thinking and writing about your feelings once is only a start to understanding your feelings and how to cope with them. Of course, not all moods are bad. Some moods are lighthearted and fun. Try not to limit your entries to only unpleasant or bad moods—remember to think about your positive moods too.

HOW DO YOU FEEL RIGHT NOW

1. What kind of mood are you in right now?

_____

_____

_____

_____

2. Describe your mood in a single word. _____

3. What are the main emotions in this mood?

_____

_____

_____

4. Put this mood into words.

a. *This mood is . . .* _____

_____

b. *If this mood had a color, it would be . . .* _____

c. *If this mood had texture, it would be . . .* _____

d. *If this mood made a noise, it would sound like . . .* _____

5. Describe your mood in more depth.

I feel . . . _____

_____

_____

_____

6. What brought this mood on?

_____

_____

_____

7. How long have you been feeling this way? Describe the cycles you've been experiencing.

_____

_____

_____

8. Is this a common mood for you? How do you feel about yourself when you're in this mood?

_____

_____

_____

9. Is this mood so strong that it's interfering with your daily life? How has it been hurting or helping your daily life?

_____

_____

_____

THINGS TO THINK ABOUT

- If this is an unpleasant mood, what can you do to avoid situations that contribute to it? If it is a pleasant mood, what sort of situations or relationships stimulate and keep it alive?
- If you've completed this entry more than once, do you have a clearer sense of your moods and what affects them?
- Have the types or frequency of your moods changed over time since your loss? In what ways?
- Are your moods so long lasting or intense that they affect your ability to function? If they are, do you feel you need help with them?

The Predictability of Feelings

As you may have discovered through the journal entries in this chapter, there are some situations that are always going to arouse certain kinds of feelings in you. Sometimes the feelings are unpleasant, but at other times a situation may evoke a warm feeling or memory.

When feelings are tied to certain kinds of situations, you can do something about them. Knowing that being around friends makes you feel safe and comfortable tells you that this is a good place to be when you're feeling anxious. On the other hand, if you know that seeing your ex-spouse produces anger or seeing your old home brings back sad and depressing memories, you're in a position to avoid those situations or at least to be prepared for how you're going to feel. Knowing your "triggers" allows you to take more control over your life.

Triggers are those things in your life that activate or arouse feelings and reactions. They can be people, sounds, smells, situations, or anything that brings back memories or feelings. Triggers that stimulate good feelings and nostalgia should be embraced, whereas triggers that evoke negative feelings should be avoided. Understanding your triggers can help you decide what to move toward and what to move away from on your healing journey.

Displacing Your Feelings

Equally predictable are the behaviors that certain feelings produce. After a bad day at work, you might feel annoyed at the pedestrian who doesn't cross the road fast enough, or you might find yourself getting easily irritated at something you hear on the news. You may go home and yell at the kids—even though you realize it's not really the kids you're mad at. On the other hand, when things are going well, you may find that everything looks good. These are examples of displaced feelings—feelings about one thing that get placed on another.

Displacement occurs when you're not even aware you're having a bad feeling or when you're trying to squash it and pretend it's not there.

At a time in your life when you're experiencing many difficult moments, feelings, and moods, it's easy to displace them onto someone or something else. Displacement occurs when you're not even aware you're having a bad feeling or when you're trying to squash the feeling and pretend it's not there. But not recognizing the feeling or choosing to ignore it doesn't make it go away. Instead, the feeling gets expressed—usually inappropriately—through displacement. You let off steam in the wrong way and probably at the wrong person. It's best to express your fears, anger, and disappointment directly. Displacing your feelings onto others—"dumping"—is not fair to them, and it keeps you away from dealing directly with the real source of your feelings.

As you complete the work in this chapter, it's important to be in touch with your feelings and how you express them. Like weather vanes, which don't explain the weather but instead show you the direction and intensity of the wind, feelings don't necessarily offer insight into why you might be feeling emotional, but they are the direct line "inside." If you stay in touch with your feelings, you'll have an important gauge to your emotional health that can help you control your emotions rather than let your emotions control you.

STAYING IN TOUCH WITH YOURSELF

1. Are there certain situations or people that trigger strong feelings in you? Who or what are they?

_____

_____

_____

_____

_____

_____

2. Are there situations or people you should go out of your way to avoid? Why?

_____

_____

_____

_____

_____

_____

3. What can you do to avoid these triggers? What alternatives are there?

_____

_____

_____

_____

_____

_____

THINGS TO THINK ABOUT

- There are bound to be some triggering situations or people you can't avoid. Are there other ways to minimize their triggering effect on you?
- Are there situations or people that really bring out the best in you? Are there ways to connect more with these?
- Are there other kinds of triggers in your life? What are they?

4. Since your separation you've experienced a lot of feelings that are negative and that perhaps interfere with your functioning. Are there also feelings you can use to help in your recovery and general sense of well-being? Explain.

_____

_____

_____

_____

_____

5. Do you displace your feelings? Onto whom, or what?

_____

_____

_____

_____

_____

6. List some ways you can find healthier or more appropriate ways to express your feelings.

_____

_____

_____

_____

THINGS TO THINK ABOUT

- What have you learned about the way you deal with feelings?
- Will you be repeating these journal entries again in order to delve into and understand your feelings in more detail? Are there entry formats that you find most helpful? Why?
- Do you think that understanding your feelings will help you deal with your divorce? In what ways?
- Do you think understanding your feelings will help you deal better with other people in your life? Who, and why?

10

Destination:
GOOD HEALTH

SUSANNAH

I went to see my family doctor three months after my separation because I felt like a wreck, emotionally and physically. I was tired all the time, I had no appetite, and I'd lost twenty pounds since Charlie left. I couldn't concentrate on anything, and I was smoking heavily. I also knew I was drinking more than I should and was starting to worry that I was developing a problem. Dr. O'Neill agreed I wasn't in good shape but ruled out any significant medical problems. But she was definitely worried and was clear that if things didn't improve for me my health might really become a problem. At that point, I was generally run down and definitely feeling depressed, but things hadn't gotten completely out of hand. She talked very honestly to me about my situation and encouraged me to let it all out. I'd known her long her enough to feel comfortable, and I did just that. I asked her what she could do for me before I fell completely apart.

We talked for a long time. She was concerned not just about my physical health, but my mental health as well. She saw them both connected to one another. We wrapped up by talking about what I could do for myself in terms of diet, exercise, and how I handle stress and relaxation. By the time I left that appointment, I understood what is meant by "wellness."

AFTER A MAJOR unwelcome change in life, it's not unusual for people to let it all go and begin to indulge themselves in all sorts of things—many of which are unhealthy—as a way to feel better or to forget. Some feel that they've been deprived enough by this loss, so why needlessly suffer more? Others let go in different ways: they stop taking care of themselves; they neglect their lives and responsibilities; or they focus in on one activity or aspect of their life, forgetting that they're still part of a larger world that has continued to exist despite their loss. Sometimes it's people's physical health that suffers; other times, their emotional health. Often it's both.

The irony, of course, is that letting go is exactly what's not called for at a time when survival depends on getting a tight grip on your life. It's not that you shouldn't occasionally self-indulge, let it all go, and take a mental vacation when things are really pressing on you emotionally. But balance and timing are critical. The letting-go behaviors, which usually reflect your emotional state, often prove more harmful than good and are generally an inadequate response to coping.

This chapter is about your physical and emotional health. It will help you explore coping with your thoughts and feelings and managing your behaviors so that you emerge from your divorce experience healthier than when you began.

Coping with What?

Although there are many different ways to describe coping, it essentially entails tolerating, managing, and eventually dealing with problems. Most people have to cope with something every day in their lives, from difficult work situations to misbehaving children to dissatisfaction with some aspect of their relationships or lives. Some people have to cope with a major physical disability or chronic pain, and others with severe life stressors such as job loss and homelessness. Often, what is most difficult to endure are the emotions that accompany the life stressor. At this time in your life, you have to cope with the loss of your marriage and all the things that may accompany the end of that relationship.

In the end, coping is more than just enduring problems. Whereas endurance involves sticking out problems and seeing them through to the end, coping goes beyond that and entails finding ways to *deal* with problems so they become less of a problem. As you work through your divorce, you'll face many things with which you'll have to contend, but most of all you'll have to find ways to cope with your own feelings.

Healthy and Unhealthy Coping

People seek out ways to cope when their feelings become overwhelming. Sometimes they will fall back into old patterns of behavior that have helped them cope in the past, patterns that may or may not have been successful.

People try to manage their feelings in ways that are both healthy and unhealthy. For instance, drinking a bottle of whiskey every day for a week after a trauma or smoking two packs of cigarettes a day when under pressure at work are both attempts to cope. They may even seem to work—people who get drunk often do forget their problems when intoxicated, and nicotine certainly does have a calming effect on people's nerves. Of course, not only don't these coping behaviors help to resolve whatever problem is causing the stress, they can often lead to a whole new set of problems. These are examples of coping styles that are both ineffective *and* unhealthy.

Healthy coping, on the other hand, both reduces the intensity of the stressor and sometimes solves the problem itself, even if not completely. The troubling situation may still hurt, upset, or bother you in some way, but its intensity is reduced, and you can move on with the daily events of your life. The feeling has receded into the background, and you're able to put it into perspective. You can either accept the situation leading to the feelings or figure out ways to resolve the problem.

Whereas endurance involves sticking out problems and seeing them through to the end, coping goes beyond that and entails finding ways to deal with problems so they actually become less of a problem.

Unlike healthy coping behaviors, which are productive, self-destructive, and self-defeating behaviors are those that get in the way of your ability to cope productively. These are also attempts to cope with a negative feeling, but the difference is that they are neither healthy nor effective ways of dealing with feelings.

In an effort to get rid of a bad feeling, instead of trying to work through and manage it, you may do things that are counterproductive. The excessive use of alcohol or drugs to drown out or numb a feeling is an example of a self-destructive behavior. It not only doesn't resolve the situation that's upsetting you, but it can also create additional problems for you. Yelling at someone on whom you rely for support and help is an example of behavior that is self-defeating. You may succeed only in pushing that person away and damaging the relationship, thus reducing the very support you need.

However, there are also many examples of healthy coping—from journal writing to physical exercise to meditation. Some people talk through their feelings. Others use art and music as a way to "soothe the savage soul." Still others may seek the company of people. The goal is for you to develop ways to cope with and manage your feelings that help, not hurt or hinder.

Healthy coping entails:

+ knowing when you have feelings—being in touch with what's going on inside

+ identifying feelings—recognizing and being able to name the feelings

+ tolerating feelings—accepting the feelings, and not trying to escape them

+ managing feelings—controlling your feelings, and not letting them control you

+ understanding feelings—connecting your feelings to their causes

HOW DO YOU COPE?

1. What are the most pressing things you have to cope with?

_____

_____

_____

_____

_____

2. What are the greatest obstacles to overcoming these things?

_____

_____

_____

_____

_____

3. In what healthy ways do you cope? Check off all that apply, and add your own.

___art   ___listening to music   ___sports

___dance   ___meditation   ___talking

___exercise   ___movies   ___therapy

___gardening   ___playing an instrument   ___walking

___hobbies   ___reading   ___writing

_____   _____   _____

_____   _____   _____

_____   _____   _____

_____   _____   _____

4. Do you ever behave self-destructively? How?

_____

_____

_____

_____

5. Do you ever behave in ways that are self-defeating? Describe some examples.

_____

_____

_____

_____

_____

6. What is your healthiest coping mechanism?

_____

_____

_____

_____

7. What is your unhealthiest coping mechanism?

_____

_____

_____

_____

THINGS TO THINK ABOUT

• What most prevents you from coping with a feeling or situation? What most helps?
• Do you keep any of your unhealthy coping mechanisms hidden from others? If so, why?

Physical Health

Following a divorce, staying emotionally healthy is an important concern. But remaining physically healthy is also important. Often, emotional and physical health are closely connected.

Poor nutrition, allowing yourself to get run down, not getting enough sleep or exercise, smoking or drinking too much, and other unhealthy physical behaviors will affect your mood, memory, ability to concentrate, tolerance level, and your mental sharpness and capacity to deal with things in general. Poor physical health can lead to poor mental health. Similarly, mental health issues affect how well people take care of themselves—a depression can lead to disturbed sleep and appetite and cause you not to care if your emotional or physical needs are being met. Of course, not taking care of yourself can lead to other real-life problems: being hungover and missing work, getting arrested for drunk driving, ceasing to take care of your children, becoming ill and possibly hospitalized, forgetting to pay bills. In short, there are real consequences to letting yourself get emotionally or physically run down.

Stress and Relaxation

Letting go and unwinding—the art of relaxation—is an important aspect of good physical and emotional health. The way we deal with stress is often critical to our ability to function effectively.

There are many ways to relax. For some people relaxation comes naturally, whereas others have to learn how to relax. Relaxation can be as simple as switching off your mind and letting your body go loose, or you might unwind by drinking a cup of hot tea or cocoa or by watching television. Some people learn simple self-hypnosis or visualization techniques. Others may take a bath, read a book, or play tapes of nature sounds or soothing music. If you're depending on alcohol, drugs, medications, or food to help you relax, consider getting some help. Your primary care physician or a professional counselor can not only help you find ways to successfully relax, but can also ensure that you're not in the process of developing habits that will only ultimately increase your problems and your level of stress.

In the next journal entry, think about your physical health and how it's affecting you—your energy, your ability to take care of things, and your mood. If you've kept in good physical shape, the entry may allow you simply to reflect on the importance of good health. It will also give you a chance to think about the connection among physical health, mental health, and relaxation. Your

Poor physical health can lead to poor mental health. . . . Letting go and unwinding— the art of relaxation —is an important aspect of good physical and emotional health.

ability to relax is good for physical and mental health; your inability to do so carries a big price tag—physical and emotional fatigue, tension and stress, worry and anxiety, and a constant state of being on the edge.

PHYSICAL HEALTH AND RELAXATION

1. Is taking care of yourself physically a problem? What kind of shape have you been in since the decision to divorce?

_____

_____

_____

_____

2. Which areas of your physical health concern you the most? Have these become concerns only recently, or have they always been a source of concern?

_____

_____

_____

_____

3. Have you been able to physically relax since your separation? If not, what prevents you from being able to relax?

_____

_____

_____

_____

4. How do you relax, or what techniques might help if you learned them? In addition to the items on the checklist, add others that do or might help. Include your use of alcohol, drugs, medications, or other potentially harmful habits. Be honest.

__breathing control	__quiet music	__sports	__walking
__cup of tea	__reading	__talking	__warm bath
__exercise	__relaxation tapes	__television	__writing
__meditation	__self-hypnosis	__visualization	__yoga

other: _____

_____

_____

5. Look back at the items you just checked off. Are any of your preferred ways to relax problematic? How do you feel about your methods?

_____

_____

_____

_____

6. What can you do to learn to relax more completely?

_____

_____

_____

_____

_____

7. What steps can you take to ensure that you're taking care of your physical health?

_____

_____

_____

_____

8. How do you view the relationship between physical health and mental health?

_____

_____

_____

_____

_____

9. What are the greatest areas of stress in your life right now?

_____

_____

_____

_____

_____

_____

THINGS TO THINK ABOUT

- Even if you don't see any problems with your physical health, do others worry about your health? How do others feel about the things you do to relax?
- What most interferes with your ability to relax? How can you overcome these obstacles?
- Do you need to change some aspects of your lifestyle in order to take better care of your health?

Developing Healthy Behaviors

Coping means using tension-relieving behaviors to help make you feel better. Even though we talk of "negative coping strategies," there's really no such thing. Negative coping behaviors are really failed attempts to cope, and generally they involve no strategy at all. Few people would seriously suggest that getting drunk every night or avoiding all future relationships are coping behaviors you should adopt. They may help temporarily deaden the pain, but they certainly won't help you overcome emotional barriers or deal with the practical realities of your new life. We may make attempts to cope in all sorts of ways—positive and negative—but, by definition, coping involves only positive and healthy behaviors.

It's pretty easy to *say* what's good for you and *name* what helps and what should be avoided. It's really hard, though, to actually *do* the things that are good for you and give up or avoid those things that aren't. It's not only hard to give up something that provides quick relief, but it's perhaps even more difficult to adopt new behaviors. For instance, if you're not an outgoing person to begin with, it will be challenging to learn how to connect with people for support. Nevertheless, it's important to be able to look at yourself and understand what makes you tick, and why. It's also imperative to know what you should be doing to make things better and what you shouldn't be doing.

Of course, you don't have to be consciously aware of your feelings or thoughts in order to behave. Most often our behaviors are simply reactions to things that involve little intentional thought. You usually don't think about and consider every aspect of your behavior before you act. Instead, you just react to the situation. These are the times, however, when your behavior may be the *wrong* response, and you realize too late that you should have thought *before* acting. Therefore it's important to devote some time to trying to understand what motivates your behavior. The ability to know when to act without thinking and when to reflect before you act is central to good decision making.

Your behaviors often are a reflection of how you feel and can say a great deal about you. Use this next journal entry to think about how you behave, and how you want to be judged by your behaviors.

The ability to know when to act without thinking and when to reflect before you act is central to good decision making.

WHAT YOU DO IS WHO YOU ARE

1. Do you ever behave in ways you later regret? Write down an example.

_____

_____

_____

_____

2. Do you ever *not* behave in ways you later wish you had? If you could change the behavior you described in Question 1, what would you do?

_____

_____

_____

3. Check off only those words that best describe your behavior since your separation. Add other adjectives in the space provided.

__aggressive   __depressed   __friendly   __rigid

__angry   __disagreeable   __insecure   __sad

__confused   __distant   __manipulative   __selfish

__considerate   __fearful   __obsessive   __sensitive

__courageous   __flexible   __outgoing   __withdrawn

other: _____   _____

_____   _____

_____   _____

4. Has your behavior changed since your separation? In what ways?

_____

_____

_____

_____

5. What behaviors do you often engage in? Check off all that apply, and add your own.

__drinking   __laughing   __walking

__drug use   __smoking   __withdrawing

__interacting with others __talking   __yelling

__ _____   __ _____   __ _____

__ _____   __ _____   __ _____

__ _____   __ _____   __ _____

__ _____   __ _____   __ _____

6. Are these behaviors you want to use and be seen using? Why or why not?

_____

_____

_____

_____

7. What message are you giving other people through your behavior? Do you mean to give that message? If you do, why?

_____

_____

_____

_____

_____

8. If your behavior has changed, why has it?

_____

_____

_____

_____

_____

9. What other changes do you want to make in your behavior?

_____

_____

_____

_____

_____

_____

THINGS TO THINK ABOUT

• People often judge you by your "outward" person—through your behavior. Is there a different "inside" person?

• Do you feel okay about your behavior? Are there changes you want or need to make?

• Do you feel okay about the way that people see you? Do you wish they could see something different? What would that be?

The Costs of Getting Relief

By now you've spent plenty of time thinking about your own feelings, behaviors, and methods for coping. You probably have a good idea of how you can help yourself deal with your feelings and an equally clear idea of what you shouldn't do (or at least what you should avoid). One of the lures of negative behaviors is that they tend to be instant tension relievers, even if they don't work in the long run. For many people it feels relaxing to have a few drinks and even better to get drunk and forget their sorrows, at least for a while. They may feel the same is true for other drugs too—feeling high quickly makes them forget their worries. Some people prefer to yell at someone or kick the dog to let off steam. Most of the negative behaviors provide instant relief, which makes them attractive. But they have big costs attached— sometimes for you *and* someone else (like the person you yelled at) and sometimes just for you.

CHECKPOINT: COPING AND GOOD HEALTH

1. What have you learned about your coping behaviors?

_____

_____

_____

_____

_____

_____

2. How do your coping behaviors work, and *why* do they work?

_____

_____

_____

_____

_____

3. Which coping methods do you most typically choose? How do these methods make you feel?

_____

_____

_____

_____

_____

4. Describe your coping behaviors. Are they positive or negative?

_____

_____

_____

_____

_____

5. How well are you coping?

_____

_____

_____

_____

_____

6. In what ways would you like to improve upon your coping skills?

_____

_____

_____

_____

_____

7. In general, how would you describe your physical health?

_____

_____

_____

_____

_____

_____

8. In general, how would you describe your mental health?

_____

_____

_____

_____

_____

THINGS TO THINK ABOUT

- Are you having special difficulties coping or changing your coping behaviors? Do you need help, either from friends or a professional therapist?
- How would you know if your coping methods were negative? Could you ask friends?
- Are you satisfied with your health, both emotional and physical?

11

Destination:
MAKING CIVIL PEACE

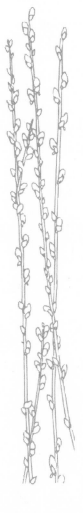

KEN

Although I thought we'd settled the divorce amicably, it seems like there's a new conflict with Anne every time I see her. One week she's telling me I'm not involved enough with the kids, and the next she's angry because I'm too controlling with their education. I don't visit the kids at her home often enough, or I'm spending too much time there. I'm not bringing the kids home on time after visits, or I'm not doing enough with them. If I get a new car for myself, I should be prepared to buy her a new one as well. Although I helped out with her college tuition, I'm not doing enough now to help with her current needs.

Anne seems to take every opportunity to pick a fight. It's like she just can't let go of her anger. I feel like I'm in a war that can't be won, and I'm getting to the point where I just don't want anything more to do with her. As soon as the kids get old enough, I'm pushing her right out of my life.

CONFLICT IS AN inevitable fact of life. Although avoiding conflict and finding peaceful ways to confront and resolve issues is a worthy goal, the fact remains that conflict exists. It's important, and necessary, to learn how to understand, tolerate, and manage conflict so that you can survive and overcome it.

The goal of conflict management in your divorce work is not to turn you into an expert manager of conflict but instead to ensure that you can walk away from your divorce in the best possible way without further conflict.

Described even in the mildest terms, a conflict implies a clash of some kind, a difference of opinion and incompatibility. Without making any value judgment about whether conflicts are "right" or "wrong," relationships of all kinds are filled with conflict. Sometimes the conflict can be resolved, sometimes not. Marriages, of course, are no exception, and when the conflict can't be resolved divorce is one possible outcome. Furthermore, generally when a marriage has failed because of a conflict of one kind or another, the divorce itself is often filled with even more conflict.

For this reason, one important part of divorce work and emotional development is learning how to understand and manage conflict so that it doesn't tear you apart. This is easier said than done. The goal of conflict management in your divorce work is not to turn you into an expert manager of conflict but instead to ensure that you can walk away from your divorce in the best possible way without further conflict.

Civil War or Civil Peace

No doubt you will continue to have some kind of relationship with your ex-spouse. It may be temporary, lasting only through the divorce proceedings ahead, or intermittent, through chance meetings in the community. You may find your relationship is longer-term because you share children, for instance, or have common interests. Depending on the nature of this ongoing relationship, it will be important to be able to tolerate one another or, even better, to actually get along. If you share friends, you'll be moving in the same social circles; if you share children, you'll probably be directly tied to one another for many years to come. After a failed marriage, you have the choice of civil war or civil peace.

If you and your ex-spouse can't deal with each other, and underlying issues continue to brew and explode periodically, every contact could be the basis for a future conflict. Things may escalate; adversarial positions may become entrenched; friends and family may take sides; and insults, litigation, threats, challenges, and bad feelings may become the order of the day—civil war.

If, however, you're able to come to terms with your difficult situation, overlook differences, and agree on rules for your interactions with one another, it will be possible to build a relationship that can work for you both. Here mutual agreement and cooperation are the order of the day—civil peace.

The next journal entry will help you to focus on what sort of relationship you want—or need—to have with your ex-spouse.

CIVIL WAR OR CIVIL PEACE

1. How has this divorce left you feeling about your ex-spouse?

_____

_____

_____

_____

_____

2. What sort of future relationship do you *want* to have with your ex-spouse?

_____

_____

_____

_____

3. What sort of future relationship do you *need* to have?

_____

_____

_____

_____

4. Who else has a stake in your relationship? Check off each stakeholder that is or will be significantly affected by this relationship, and add others who are relevant. Briefly note how they will be affected by a civil war or a civil peace.

Stakeholder   *Effect on this Stakeholder*

children   _____

coworkers   _____

community members   _____

family   _____

friends   _____

in-laws   _____

neighbors   _____

_____   _____

_____   _____

5. What issues will you need to overcome in order to pursue civil peace?

_____

_____

_____

6. What issues will need to be overcome for your ex-spouse to pursue civil peace?

_____

_____

_____

7. How important is a civil peace to you? Explain why.

_____

_____

_____

8. What are the consequences of a civil war? How would it affect you or your children?

_____

_____

_____

- Who will most suffer if your relationship is based on a civil war? Who will benefit most from a civil peace?
- Can you really afford a civil war? Is this how you want to live your life?
- What most prevents you from actively pursuing civil peace?

Resolving Conflict

Some people seem to thrive on conflict, whereas others try to walk away from it. In some couples, one person is conflict driven and the other conflict aversive. Sometimes both are drawn to clashes, and sometimes both shy away from confrontation. Neither approach is right. Where the objective is a mutually satisfactory resolution to issues, it's the outcome that determines which style is most effective.

If you or your ex-spouse is conflict prone and the other conflict shy, divorce issues may be driven by the conflict seeker and take on a challenging or adversarial flavor.

If you or your ex-spouse is conflict prone and the other conflict shy, divorce issues may be driven by the conflict seeker and take on a challenging or adversarial flavor. If one of you seeks solutions through challenge, conflicts may be provoked. If you're both conflict driven, get ready for a big battle. If both of you are conflict aversive, you may fail to resolve important issues. It's critical that you learn how to recognize, address, and resolve difficulties.

The first task dealing with conflict is to stop pretending it doesn't exist. Although it might be desirable to eliminate conflict entirely, the more realistic task is to learn to manage and resolve differences. Learning how to handle confrontation and resolve conflict will allow you to move toward a relationship that ultimately can best serve you and your ex-spouse in your new roles as divorced partners.

Conflict resolution usually entails four steps.

1. *Conflict recognition.* To resolve conflict you first have to recognize you're in a conflict or heading for one. That's usually the easy part, though not always. Sometimes conflicts are hidden. Sometimes they are expressed in ways that deflect

your focus from the true nature of the conflict. As a result, the underlying issues remain brewing beneath the surface.

2. *Conflict management*. Once recognized, you must be able to *manage* the conflict so that it doesn't explode into an angry altercation that can push you farther apart or damage a newly revised version of your relationship. For instance, if you're the divorced parents of a young child, you won't want to compromise your ability to work together in your child's best interests. Nor do you want to push the conflict back beneath the surface and allow it to erupt again.

3. *Conflict understanding*. Many conflicts seem to drag on, even though individual skirmishes get settled. If you understand the roots and nature of the conflict, your attempts at resolution will be aimed at the right problem.

4. *Conflict resolution*. Resolving a conflict means addressing and settling the root causes of the problem. This requires the ability to see things from more than one perspective.

The next journal entry will help you to think about and focus on a single conflict. However, as you complete it think about how this particular conflict is connected to other conflicts in your relationship. Focus on yourself: what do *you* need to do to improve the situation and work toward conflict resolution? Since this entry is designed to address only a single conflict, photocopy the blank form so that you can use it to work through other conflicts.

UNDERSTANDING THE ISSUES

1. Describe a current conflict or clash with your ex-spouse.

_____

_____

_____

_____

_____

2. For how long have you known this conflict was coming? Has it been brewing for a while, or did it come out of the blue? Explain the circumstances of both sides of the conflict.

_____

_____

_____

_____

_____

3. How are you affected by this conflict?

_____

_____

_____

_____

_____

4. What do you need to do to ensure the conflict doesn't escalate further, or disappear unresolved?

_____

_____

_____

_____

_____

5. What are the root causes of this conflict? In what way is this conflict connected to an older problem or pattern of interactions?

_____

_____

_____

_____

6. Are the current issues in this particular conflict the real issues, or is there something else going on? What is the real issue at play in this conflict?

_____

_____

_____

7. What can most help to resolve the real issues at stake here, at least minimally?

_____

_____

_____

_____

8. What can *you* do to get this conflict resolved and move on?

_____

_____

_____

_____

9. What should you avoid doing that might otherwise deepen the conflict?

_____

_____

_____

_____

THINGS TO THINK ABOUT

- Who is most affected by this conflict, you or your ex-spouse? Who else is affected, and in what ways?
- In what important ways are you contributing to the conflict rather than the resolution? In what ways can you change to facilitate peace, not war? What stops you from changing?
- How important is it to resolve issues at stake in this conflict? What will happen if you don't resolve the conflict? How might things deteriorate further?

Gains and Losses

Unresolved conflicts and the failure to win peace following a divorce often mean the loss of something. In perhaps the most critical instance, it can, to the detriment of the children, spell the loss of a cooperative parental relationship. It can mean the loss of in-laws or friends who came to be part of your close circle, or it may mean you feel uncomfortable going to a favorite social spot because it's frequented by your ex-spouse. If you're tied to your ex-spouse, even after divorce, through children or shared relationships with in-laws or common friends, there'll always be special occasions and gatherings that one or the other will not be able to attend because of an inability to be in the same place at the same time. Under different circumstances, unresolved conflicts may result in the loss of income or property. It may even be the loss of a genuine friendship between you and your ex-spouse that might have developed had you both been able to build a peace.

The gains are the mirror image of these losses. If you and your ex-spouse have grown adept at resolving conflicts, you'll be able to amicably work out whose home your children visit on the holidays and together be able to attend and celebrate your children's victories and special moments. You'll be able to continue family ties you've developed with in-laws, even if they've taken a turn in direction, and spend time with friends who know and like you both. You'll be able to settle legal, financial, and property differences without going to court, and you'll be able to run into one another at the supermarket without hastily heading for the exit. You may even be able to appreciate one another for the very things that brought you together in the first place.

Resolving differences doesn't mean saying you were wrong; yielding doesn't mean giving in; and compromising doesn't mean surrendering. By seeking a civil peace you are, at the very least, avoiding a civil war.

Resolving differences doesn't mean saying you were wrong; yielding doesn't mean giving in; and compromising doesn't mean surrendering. By seeking a civil peace you are, at the very least, avoiding a civil war. On the middle ground, you're accepting your losses and moving on with a new life, unfettered by hostility. At best, you're recognizing your differences, growing, and using old ties to build a new future.

Sometimes you have to think about what you can *lose* in order to realize what you might *gain*. The next entry will give you the chance to think about gains and losses, and which are more important to you.

GAINS

1. Name five reasons to get or stay angry with your ex-spouse.

a. _____

b. _____

c. _____

d. _____

e. _____

2. Name five reasons for your ex-spouse to get or stay angry with you.

a. _____

b. _____

c. _____

d. _____

e. _____

3. Check off every reason to build a peace, and add six more of your own.

__children   __in-law relationships   __religious/spiritual beliefs

__financial stability   __lifestyle stability   __shared friends

__friendship with my ex-spouse   __peace of mind   __sharing special occasions

a. _____   d. _____

b. _____   e. _____

c. _____   f. _____

4. What are more important to you—the reasons to be angry or the reasons to build a peace?

_____

_____

_____

_____

_____

5. Which do you think are more important to your ex-spouse? Why?

_____

_____

_____

_____

6. What can you do to overcome your anger at your ex-spouse?

_____

_____

_____

_____

7. What can you do to help your ex-spouse overcome his or her anger at you?

_____

_____

_____

_____

8. What will you lose in a civil war?

_____

_____

_____

_____

9. What must *you* do to work toward civil peace?

_____

_____

_____

_____

_____

_____

THINGS TO THINK ABOUT

• What sort of help might you need to overcome whatever stops you from seeking peace?

• Do you feel that civil peace implies forgiveness or that you've forgotten transgressions?

Finding Peace

Seeking peaceful solutions doesn't mean turning your back on important issues or shying away from problems that must be resolved. It simply means finding ways to resolve conflicts that don't open up old wounds, create new ones, or throw fuel on the fire. Seeking peace does not imply passivity; being assertive is not the same as being aggressive.

You may have many issues to confront and resolve. Some will be handled with relative ease and will not resurface once resolved (e.g., who lives where, who gets the CD collection). Other issues will be more enduring, and their resolutions may require periodic adjustments (e.g., child support payments, child rearing in general, how you treat one another when you meet). And just because you may be civil and seek cooperation, it doesn't mean your ex-spouse will see things the same way. You may need to find other ways to get your ex-spouse to work with you.

Use the next journal entry to think about important issues and the lengths to which you're prepared to go to get them resolved. Although solutions offered on the checklist in the entry are primarily "peaceful," some are more adversarial than others. The goal of this entry, however, is to help you think about the sort of choices available to you and the price you may have to pay for any choice you make.

MEANS AND ENDS

1. List up to five issues that are now or will be important to resolve.

a. _____

b. _____

c. _____

d. _____

e. _____

2. Pick one of these issues as the subject of the entry.

_____

3. Check off three routes you can take to resolve this situation and more choices of your own. Rank in order your choices, with 1 as your most preferred choice.

__arbitration   __court order   __mediation

__compromise   __friends acting as go-between   __personal discussion

__counseling   __legal action   __personal favor

other: _____   _____

_____   _____

_____   _____

4. What's the downside to the primary choice you made?

_____

_____

_____

5. Which choice offers the greatest promise of mutual satisfaction? Why?

_____

_____

6. Which of your choices is likely to increase the tension and problems between you?

_____

7. Given the relative importance of this issue to you, to what extremes are you prepared to go to resolve this issue in your favor?

_____

_____

_____

_____

THINGS TO THINK ABOUT

- Is your ex-spouse someone who's simply not willing to compromise, no matter what you do? In this case, how can you pursue a civil peace?
- Are there some issues just not worth fighting over?
- Are you thinking about all you can lose when you make decisions to win an issue in your favor?

Being Civil

Being on civil terms has its own rewards. Sharing your child's graduation, confirmation, wedding, or other special event is an experience you both can relish if you have a civil peace.

Finally, civil peace isn't just about resolving problems and managing conflict. It's also about how you treat one another generally—when you meet at a party, when your ex-spouse comes up in conversation, or when you drop off the kids for visitation with their other parent. Are you cold or aloof, snappy and critical, or friendly and engaged? Obviously, your reactions and responses to one another can run the gamut. Even if you're initially on good terms with one another following the initial decision to separate, the process of divorce can turn things around.

Being on civil terms has its own rewards. Sharing your child's graduation, confirmation, wedding, or other special event is an experience you both can relish if you have a civil peace. There are probably few quicker ways to alienate your children than to ruin *their* special occasions because of *your* civil war. If you or your ex-spouse remarries, will your civil war spill over to the new spouse also? How about when you each run into your former in-laws or friends?

CHECKPOINT: CIVILITY

1. How do you generally treat your ex-spouse when you meet?

_____

_____

_____

_____

2. How does your ex-spouse treat you?

_____

_____

_____

_____

3. What relationship do you want to have with your ex-spouse as you each move on with your respective lives?

_____

_____

_____

_____

4. What's the most difficult aspect of being civil to your ex-spouse?

_____

_____

_____

_____

5. Can you maintain a civil relationship? What are some ways you can keep things civilized?

_____

_____

_____

_____

6. Review your journal entries in this chapter. How important is it to maintain or pursue civil peace?

_____

_____

_____

_____

_____

THINGS TO THINK ABOUT

- What does it actually mean to you to be "civil?"
- Do your plans to be civil vanish when you're confronted with the reality of actually seeing your ex-spouse? What can you do to change this situation?
- Is it difficult to even think about being civil to your ex-spouse? What will it take for you to change your perspective? Do you want to change it?
- What's the price of not having a civil relationship? Are you willing to pay that price?

12

Destination:

REDEFINING RELATIONSHIPS

ELIZABETH

After the divorce, I just couldn't stand to see Dan. I wanted him out of my life, but he wasn't and couldn't be because we had three kids whom he saw regularly. The worst part was that I still wanted to be part of the family I'd found through Dan. I'd quickly come to feel close to his dad and his two sisters, I enjoyed Dan's large extended family, and they'd all accepted me just as easily. On the surface, none of that had changed after the divorce, and I still saw them regularly because of the kids. I went to all the family gatherings, and I spent social time with his sisters who'd long ago become friends of mine. But, little by little, I realized that these actually weren't healthy relationships for me to have.

I couldn't talk to any of them about how angry I was with Dan or how irresponsible he was as a divorced parent, because they just didn't want to hear. And, although I longed to hear them tell me that I was right, that I was their favorite one, not Dan, I knew this could never happen. It took me a while, but I finally realized that I had to give up this yearning to replace Dan in his family, and move away from these relationships. That was like getting divorced again, but it was probably one of the personally healthiest decisions I've made.

ONE OF THE most important relationships in your life has ended. At first it may seem that no relationship can occupy the place once filled by your marriage and your partner. And that's normal. After all, no two relationships are alike, and comparing relationships with different people is like comparing apples with oranges. The goal in your divorce work is neither to "replace" your ex-spouse nor to push every aspect of that old relationship out of your life.

As you move on to the third stage of your divorce work, by redefining and often restructuring *existing* relationships, especially those connected in some way to your former marriage, you engage in the tasks of reorganizing your life.

In this chapter you'll have the opportunity to think about your current relationships and what you want and don't want from them.

Existing Relationships

Of the relationships already in your life, you have two kinds: those that predate your marriage or are somehow independent of it and those that are linked to your marriage. The first category comprises members of your own family, your own friends, co-workers, and other relationships that aren't dependent of any way on your marriage. In the second category, you have relationships that are closely linked to your marriage. Members of this category include in-laws and shared friends, for example. The relationships in the latter category may be less resilient than those in the former and often dissipate after your divorce. However, if you have children, some of your marriage-connected relationships, including your relationship with the other parent, will be permanent, even if you wish they weren't. Although *you're* divorced from your ex-spouse and your in-laws, your children aren't. They remain a *permanent* part of your ex-spouse's family.

After your separation, existing relationships will start to be redefined, especially those that are in some way attached to your

Although you're divorced from your ex-spouse and your in-laws, your children aren't.

marriage. Over time, these relationships may grow stronger or weaker; you may become closer to some people while drifting away from others. Some of these existing relationships may take on an awkward or uncomfortable quality. Others may prove comforting and supportive and become increasingly important. Regardless of the nature and history of the relationships linked to or predating your marriage, these are the ones that will begin to change and almost at once.

Redefining Relationships

In some of your existing relationships, you have a great deal of control over who you choose to see and who you don't. But this isn't always the case. You may, for example, want a relationship to continue with someone, but the relationship itself proves too emotionally charged or awkward for everyone involved. And, sometimes ending a relationship you're not inclined to continue is impossible. For instance, even if you prefer not to have any contact with your ex-spouse or former in-laws if children are involved, reality dictates that it will be impossible to end those relationships. There will always be times when you have to drop off or pick up your kids at your ex-spouse's family functions or special occasions, and there will always be decisions about your children's future that involve other family members. In most cases, it's not only very important for your children to spend time with you *two* as parents, it's also important for them to maintain ties with both sides of their family. Your issues with your ex-spouse and/or your former in-laws shouldn't interfere with those relationships, unless there's the possibility of some kind of harm to the children. In some cases, you may not have any choice at all. Visits with the other parent, as well as contact with grandparents, may be court ordered.

There are some relationships in which the other person wants change. In fact, this may be reminiscent of your divorce itself, if it was your spouse's idea to separate. Sometimes the other person may seem disinterested or unavailable. Or you may feel as though

It's not only very important for your children to spend time with you two as parents, it's also important for them to maintain ties with both sides of their family.

you've been dropped by the other person who no longer feels comfortable in your company. Some relationships, then, will be redefined by their circumstances and by what the other person wants. But for many of your existing relationships the issue of what you want and don't want is quite instrumental in defining where the relationships go. Even if you must maintain a relationship with your ex-spouse and former in-laws, you're still in a position to decide the kind of contact you want to have and how you want this relationship to be structured. In such "mandated" relationships, your choices about the quality and quantity of contact will hopefully be guided by a win-win philosophy.

In the case of "nonrequired" relationships—those over which you *can* exercise a great deal of personal choice—you're free to define for yourself what you want. In some cases, you may definitely want change. In some cases you may simply not want to maintain the relationship at all. In other cases you may decide to refocus relationships by tackling issues head on and talking openly about the divorce and how it's affected that particular relationship.

Your divorce will also affect existing relationships that are independent of your marriage. Sometimes mutual friends may avoid you because they feel awkward spending time with you or feel they have to choose sides. From some family members and friends you may receive increased sympathy and concern. From people who never approved of your marriage in the first place, you may get a patronizing "I told you so," which will shape your feelings and relationship with them. You may feel a greater need to spend time with family and old friends or completely redefine old relationships, or shed your old life altogether.

In other words, your view of and experience with all your existing relationships may well have changed by the end of your marriage. For that reason, the redefinition of these relationships —deciding what they're to become—is *your* job. Redefining relationships is a key task of the third stage of your divorce work. This stage entails making active decisions about ending some relationships or significantly reworking them so that contact is limited. In other relationships, redefining may involve openly discussing the situation and clearing the air. Sometimes maintaining a relationship will require no discussion at all.

Exploring relationships through journal writing is one way to gain insight into your needs and set new directions for yourself.

A QUICK LOOK AT RELATIONSHIPS

1. Check off existing relationships that have been significant in your life, and rate how important each relationship is to you. Think about groups of people (such as friends or in-laws,) rather than focusing on specific individuals. Skip any categories that don't apply to you, and add other relationships to the checklist.

Type of Relationship	Level of Importance				
	Not	Minimally	Undecided	Somewhat	Very
children	___	___	___	___	___
community	___	___	___	___	___
coworkers	___	___	___	___	___
ex-spouse	___	___	___	___	___
in-laws	___	___	___	___	___
my own family	___	___	___	___	___
my own friends	___	___	___	___	___
neighbors	___	___	___	___	___
shared friends	___	___	___	___	___
spouse's friends	___	___	___	___	___
stepchildren	___	___	___	___	___
support group	___	___	___	___	___
other: _____					

_____

_____

_____

2. Reflect back on the relationship list you just created. Now carefully think about the sentence starts below, and complete them with candor and honesty, even if you don't like the answers.

a. *My relationships are . . .* _____

_____

b. *When I think of the sort of relationships I have, I . . .* _____

_____

c. *With my relationships, I most need to work on . . .* _____

_____

d. *If there's one thing I need to change in my relationships, it's . .* _____

_____

e. *When it comes to my relationships, I need . . .* _____

_____

3. What's the best thing about your current relationships?

_____

_____

_____

_____

4. What's the worst thing about your current relationships?

_____

_____

_____

THINGS TO THINK ABOUT
- What was the most difficult part of this entry? What was most satisfying?
- Overall, are you satisfied or dissatisfied with your relationships? Do you need to work to improve or make changes in your relationships?
- What did you learn from this entry?
- Was it difficult or painful to think honestly about your relationships? How honest were you?

The Good Relationships, the Bad, and Those in Need of Change

First think of current relationships that you find unsatisfying, uncomfortable, or awkward. These are the relationships you'd like to end or significantly change.

The next three entries provide blank formats to work through three distinct kinds of existing relationships. These are:

1. those relationships you'd like to discontinue but either can't or haven't
2. those relationships that you want to stick with but need some serious readjustment to better fit your needs
3. those relationships that you'd like to develop further

Each entry will focus your thoughts on a single relationship. Think about which relationships are most pressing right now, and work on those. You are not limited to writing about one relationship, and you may want to copy these entries to evaluate other relationships at a later time. You may also want to return to these journal entries weeks or months from now, and use them to think about and address relationship issues and choices that have developed and still are developing.

THE BAD

1. Which relationship are you describing in this entry?

_____

2. What is it about this relationship that you find the most uncomfortable or dislike the most?

_____

_____

_____

_____

_____

3. How much do your feelings about how you've been treated in this relationship affect your decision to stay with or discontinue the relationship?

_____

_____

_____

_____

_____

4. Why do you remain in the relationship?

_____

_____

_____

_____

_____

5. What prevents you from ending or changing the relationship?

_____

_____

_____

_____

_____

6. If you can't end or change this relationship, how can you better tolerate it?

_____

_____

_____

_____

7. What three things can you do to change or restructure this relationship?

a. _____

b. _____

c. _____

- Are there legitimate explanations for why you remain in this relationship? If not, are you making excuses for not ending or significantly changing it?
- Do you get *something* out of this relationship? What? What would your life be like without this relationship?
- Are you being honest with yourself?

Improving Relationships

Many of your relationships may be important and satisfying for any number of reasons but may nevertheless need changes to make them work better and fit your needs as well as the needs of the other person in the relationship.

For the next journal entry, focus on a worthwhile relationship that nevertheless requires some kind of modification to make it generally more satisfying. Think about why you want to stay in this relationship, the changes that will have to take place to make it more satisfying, and what's stopping you from introducing the changes. As your relationships are often more a reflection of you than the other party, this journal entry presents the opportunity to think about yourself as well as your relationships.

TO CHANGE

1. Which relationship are you describing in this entry?

_____

2. What is it that keeps you or makes you want to stay in this relationship?

_____

_____

_____

_____

_____

_____

3. Describe three things that would most improve this relationship, or make it better fit your needs.

a. _____

b. _____

c. _____

4. Describe three things that you can do to improve this relationship.

a. _____

b. _____

c. _____

5. What prevents you from bringing changes into this relationship?

_____

_____

_____

_____

6. What do you most *want* from this relationship?

_____

_____

_____

_____

7. What do you most *need* from this relationship?

_____

_____

_____

_____

8. What does this relationship say about *you*?

_____

_____

_____

9. What's the future of this relationship without necessary change or growth?

_____

_____

_____

The "Keepers"

"Keepers" are those relationships that you definitely want to maintain or improve on. Some of these relationship choices will be made for healthy reasons. You care for that person and feel cared for. This person has, and will be, important in your life, or this is simply a fun and pleasant relationship that lifts your spirits. Perhaps it's a relationship that you hope will develop further and evolve into something more meaningful, and even romantic.

You may also be making relationship decisions for less than healthy or honest reasons. You want this person to validate *you,* not your ex-spouse. Perhaps you simply want to feel loved by someone, even if it happens to be the wrong person. There are as many unhealthy reasons to maintain a relationship as there are healthy ones. The goal for you is to know the difference and understand your motivations as you redefine and make relationship choices.

The following entry can be used repeatedly for those relationships that are on your mind and need reflective thought and resolution. Remember, you can return to any of these entry formats months from now to reexamine the same relationship over time or other relationship issues and choices that have yet to develop.

There are as many unhealthy reasons to maintain a relationship as there are healthy ones. The goal for you is to know the difference and understand your motivations as you redefine and make relationship choices.

WHAT DO YOU WANT FROM THIS RELATIONSHIP?

1. Which relationship are you describing in this entry?

_____

2. Why is this a relationship you want to keep?

_____

_____

_____

_____

3. What do you want from this particular relationship? Check off every answer that reflects the reasons you choose to stay in this relationship or what you hope to get from it. Think hard and honestly about your answers here, adding other reasons of your own.

__comfort and nurture

__connection to my past

__emotional security and stability

__financial security and stability

__help for my children

__love and affection

__make my ex-spouse sorry

__personal growth

__personal support

__personal validation

__possibility of romance

__proof that I was right, not my ex-spouse

__proof of my self-worth

__safety

__self-esteem

__sense of belonging

__someone to take my side

__snub or hurt my ex-spouse

__staying connected to a family

__what's best for my children

other: _____

_____

_____

_____

4. Look back at the answers you checked off. Which is the closest to your *primary* reason for wanting this relationship?

_____

5. Do your reasons reflect a healthy or unhealthy foundation for this relationship?

_____

_____

_____

6. What are the downsides of this relationship?

_____

_____

_____

_____

_____

7. What is it you *need* from this relationship?

_____

_____

_____

_____

_____

8. Can you get what you need? Given what you know, can this relationship take you where you need to go? How?

_____

_____

_____

_____

_____

9. How best can you deal with or redefine this relationship?

_____

_____

_____

_____

THINGS TO THINK ABOUT

- Is this a realistic relationship for you? Can your needs and expectations be reasonably met by this relationship?
- Are you looking at this relationship and your needs honestly?
- Does this relationship have built-in conflicts that are bound to lead to disappointment and failure later on? What are the conflicts for you? What are the conflicts for the other person?
- How can you best build on this relationship?

Authentic Relationships

As you pursue and develop new relationships, especially intimate ones, it'll be important to think about what you want and why you want it. One risk in building new relationships after the breakup of a marriage is that the new relationship is intended only as a substitute for your ex-spouse, as something to fill a void or need in your life or as a snub to your ex-spouse. New relationships built on that sort of basis are not likely to develop far, develop successfully, or fill a genuine need for intimacy. They're not fair to you, and they're certainly not fair to the other person in the relationship.

The most satisfying relationships are those that are authentic *— relationships that are honest and clear, with a genuine concern for the needs of both people in the relationship.*

The most satisfying relationships are those that are *authentic* —relationships that are honest and clear, with a genuine concern for the needs of both people in the relationship. Although honest relationships don't guarantee success, they do at least ensure the best chance for positive interactions and outcomes. At this time in your life, at the end of a relationship that *didn't* work, you have the chance to redefine and develop relationships that *do* work.

CHECKPOINT: RELATIONSHIPS

1. How satisfied are you with your current relationships?

_____

_____

_____

_____

_____

2. What do you most want from your existing relationships?

_____

_____

_____

_____

_____

3. How do you want to be treated by people in your current relationships?

_____

_____

_____

_____

4. Who can you most depend on in your current relationships?

_____

_____

_____

_____

5. How can you tell which relationships are best avoided over time?

_____

_____

_____

_____

6. How can you best deal with existing relationships?

_____

_____

_____

7. How can you best get your needs met from existing relationships?

_____

_____

_____

8. If you have kids, how can you best deal with relationships that involve them?

_____

_____

_____

_____

9. What do you most need to do to best handle existing relationships?

_____

_____

_____

_____

THINGS TO THINK ABOUT

- As you've reflected on your existing relationships, what have you learned about yourself?
- Are you seeing your relationships and where they're going clearly? Are there difficult relationship choices to be made? How will you find the strength and support to make necessary changes?
- What will your life be like if you actually take the lead in redefining current relationships? Will it be fuller or emptier?
- Have these entries changed the way you view your relationships? If so, in what way? Will you continue to use these journaling entries over time to deal with developments in relationships?

13

Destination:

SEEING WITH NEW EYES

MARK

I got to the point where I felt stuck in a rut, trapped in the same old thinking with the same old problems. Although my whole life had changed after the divorce, nothing really seemed to be very different. Even though I felt ready to move on with my new single life, I still felt like the same old person, seeing things the same old way.

I finally realized that I had to find ways to start looking at my life and seeing things in it in a different way. Without a personal makeover of the way I was thinking, nothing was going to change. I started reading books on self-improvement, took a fitness class, and started tennis lessons. I began to do things I hadn't done before. I began to change my daily routine and started seeing things a little differently. After a while I felt like I was breaking through the barriers I'd created for myself.

ONCE THE INITIAL shock of a trauma, personal crisis, or other significant life changing event passes, people tend to start seeing things differently. The familiar world seems less so. Sometimes things that were once important to you lose meaning, and at other times the things you believed in have become unclear or begin to disintegrate. Your assumptions about your world begin

to come undone. In this chapter you'll be exposed to new ways of seeing yourself and seeing the world around you. During this process, you'll have the opportunity to see things through fresh eyes and use this new view as the cornerstone on which to reconstruct your system of values and beliefs.

Finding Inspiration

Sometimes seeing things through fresh eyes requires a little help. Seeing things through other people's eyes can help activate your own ideas. At some point in your life, you've no doubt had the experience of reading a passage in a book or hearing some song lyrics that seem to capture precisely how you're feeling and push you into action. A verse or a quotation—from a poem, song, book, or speech—can contain tremendous power.

Because they often contain pearls of wisdom, quotations can help you understand how you're feeling, offer a new view of the world, help simplify confusing situations, and offer guidance and direction. In short, in just a few words quotations can eloquently inform and inspire.

For the following entry, pick three quotations or inspirational words that have particular meaning for you or move you in some way. You can find these almost anywhere—in collected volumes that contain nothing but quotations, in stories or poems you've read, in lyrics, or in someone else's spoken word. Before you begin to work on your next entry, think about some of your favorite passages. You may wish to seek them out in preparation for the journal entry. Because this is an entry that you may want to repeat using different quotations, make copies of the blank entry before completing it.

WORDS OF WISDOM

1. Select three favorite or otherwise meaningful quotations, and copy each one here.

a. _____

b. _____

c. _____

2. For this entry, pick one of these quotations to focus on.

3. Why did you select this particular quotation for this entry?

_____

_____

_____

4. How do these words have relevance to your life at this time?

_____

_____

_____

_____

_____

5. What do these words mean to you?

_____

_____

_____

_____

_____

6. In what ways can these words instruct or offer you direction?

_____

_____

_____

_____

_____

Looking Inside

It's a common aspiration in many cultures, ancient and modern, to "know thyself." There are many routes to this sort of introspection and internal reflection—quiet meditation, a walk through nature, private musings about the world, or listening to music. For some, a solitary sport like running, swimming, or bicycling offers a perfect forum for developing internal awareness. For others, fine arts such as painting, photography, or dance serves as a focal point for directing attention inward. For still others, becoming engrossed in a book or a poem provides a way into the ideas and words of another and a retreat from the world outside.

Being contemplative means slowing down and stopping the activities of your everyday life so that you can look at and consider the things that surround you, discover for yourself what works best for you, and simply think about things that may have no answers.

Whichever route you take, the objective is to focus the mind on itself. Despite the activity you choose, the process is one of contemplation: exploring feelings without becoming passionate, considering the world without taking action, and speaking to yourself without words. Being contemplative means slowing down and stopping the activities of your everyday life so that you can look at and consider the things that surround you, discover for yourself what works best for you, and simply think about things that may have no answers. Introspection helps you to know yourself and to understand how you affect and are affected by the world outside.

Not everyone is naturally contemplative, however. For some, slowing down and thinking in this way is not a part of their normal way of doing things. Nevertheless, it's important to learn new ways of approaching and interacting with the world. This period of enormous change in your life may be one of those times when the act and art of contemplation is exactly what's needed to help reconstruct and reinvent your life.

Slowing Down the World

For many people, slowing down is easier said than done. We live in a world geared for speed: fast cars and jets transport us from one place to another, television covers events as they're happening, and Internet access provides us with instant communication. Even the practical and emotional changes you're now experiencing are happening rapidly and perhaps outside your control. Walking is one way to slow down and help you get back in control—not "power walking" which is intended for exercise, but slow, contemplative walking, where one can get away from the fast pace of life.

The next journal entry will help you to slow down and discover what's around you. It can help you to see things that you normally may not notice because you simply aren't looking for them. This entry is intended to direct your attention to both the outward *and* the inward. You will learn to use your environment to help you find ways to think in new and refreshing ways. The entry takes you on a walking route of your choice. You might choose a crowded city street on a bright spring day; a windy beach in the early morning; or a favorite trail. Any environment is interesting if you open your senses and mind to it. Wherever you choose to go, go alone.

Plan to spend at least thirty minutes on your walk. Walk slowly, and think about yourself and your surroundings. Observe the sights, sounds, and smells. Take a notebook and pen with you. If you like to draw, bring a sketchbook; if you enjoy photography, a camera. If you look, listen, and think, you'll notice all sorts of things that you haven't seen before. You'll find a way to tune in to those ordinary things around you that can provide pleasure, comfort, and meaning. If you can apply these skills on your walk, you can learn to use them in your everyday life as well.

Read the questions posed in the next journal entry *before* you leave for your walk. After your walk, complete the following journal entry.

USING YOUR FEET TO OPEN YOUR EYES

1. Where did you walk?

_____

_____

_____

_____

2. Think about the environment in which you walked. Describe your walk as you might to someone who has never had the opportunity to take such a walk.

a. *I walked among . . .* _____

_____

b. *I was surrounded by . . .* _____

_____

c. *On my walk, I saw . . .* _____

_____

d. *The ground beneath my feet felt . . .* _____

_____

e. *The sounds around me were . . .* _____

_____

f. *I was most struck by . . .* _____

_____

3. Stop along the way and find somewhere to sit. Observe what's going on around you.

a. If you were in a public place, what were other people doing? If in a private spot, away from all people, what was going on around you?

_____

_____

_____

_____

b. Describe at least one interesting observation of another person or interaction between people. If alone, describe at least one thing in your environment that was interesting to you.

_____

_____

_____

_____

c. If you walked in a constructed environment, like a city or park, describe at least one interesting architectural feature of a building or structure you saw. If you were in a natural environment like woods or on a beach, describe at least one naturally occurring feature that stood out as unusual or especially interesting.

_____

_____

_____

_____

4. Describe the weather that day. How did it affect your mood?

_____

_____

_____

_____

5. What two colors really stood out for you for you? Describe them as you would to someone who can only see the world in black and white.

_____

_____

_____

_____

6. Along your walk, stop at least twice, close your eyes, and listen to the sounds around you.

a. Describe the sounds that most immediately surrounded you.

_____

_____

_____

_____

b. Describe the sounds in the far distance or in the deep background.

_____

_____

_____

_____

7. What odors were carried in the air? Were they familiar smells? What did they make you think of?

_____

_____

_____

_____

8. Did any special thoughts, questions, or answers emerge as you walked?

_____

_____

_____

_____

9. Describe your overall experience on this walk.

_____

_____

_____

_____

10. What did you see that you'd never seen before?

_____

_____

_____

_____

11. What did you think about that you'd never thought about before?

_____

_____

_____

_____

THINGS TO THINK ABOUT

- Will you take another contemplative walk? Will you make walks like this part of your regular routine?
- Are there other places to take a similar walk in which you pay attention to things that you've never noticed before?
- Did your walk slow you down and open your mind? What have you learned from this experience?

Exploring Your Life

In many ways, the essence of contemplation is the deliberate study of the old in order to find something new. Within your own life, there are probably many unexplored corners—things you've never noticed or thought about—and many clues to how you've lived your life and how you want to live it now. The journal entries in this chapter are intended to help you stop and consider your life and the things within it and outside of it.

One way to become more aware of your life and what's going on around and inside you is to find time each day to stop and think. The next journal entry provides a means for a daily search of your life and an opportunity to reflect each day on what you've learned about yourself from that search. You'll build a portrait of yourself over a period of seven days, based on the things in your daily life. Each day you'll embark on a search within your everyday life for those things that are always there but that you don't usually see, opening your eyes to those things hidden in the corners of your life.

One way to become more aware of your life and what's going on around and inside you is to find time each day to stop and think.

The exercise runs over a seven-day period. You'll need a small notebook that you can easily keep with you during the day to jot down your thoughts and your discoveries as you search for each item. You'll also need a small camera that you can carry with you each day. You'll conclude each day with a written journal entry that summarizes your feelings.

For each day of the seven days find:

- Something important in your life. Find something in your *daily* life that has special meaning to you: a possession or article of clothing, jewelry or a memento of some kind, a photograph or painting, or an important event or ritual that's part of your everyday life.

- An interesting corner of your life. Find some physical aspect of your life that's always there but that you seldom normally see because you're not looking for it: a fascinating play of light and shadow through a window, the way the trees outside your window move in the breeze, the way two walls in your home or office intersect, or the pattern on an armchair.

- A token or symbol of your life. Find something in your life that serves as a symbol of who you are, your identity, or your achievements. This could be something you intentionally wear or carry each day to make a statement about yourself or your beliefs or something that unintentionally says something about you or your life.

- A photograph of your life. For each day of this journal entry, take one photograph. Your goal is to see things through creative eyes and to look for an opportunity each day to take a snapshot of something in your life that moves you or says something about you and your life.

- A choice in your life. As you move through your days, you make choices, many without thought. During this journal exercise, consider the choices you're making—such as drinking an extra cup of coffee or staying an extra hour at work.

- A reflection about your life. The daily journal entry ends each day with an observation about yourself and what you've learned from the search of your life you've conducted that day.

At the completion of the seven days, write a concluding entry that summarizes your experience with this journal entry. This is a journal entry that you may wish to repeat, so photocopy it and save it for a future time.

A SELF-PORTRAIT

DAY 1

Something important in my life: _____

An interesting corner of my life: _____

A token or symbol of my life: _____

A photograph of my life: _____

A choice in my life: _____

Reflection on my search for this day: _____

_____

_____

_____

_____

DAY 2

Something important in my life: _____

An interesting corner of my life: _____

A token or symbol of my life: _____

A photograph of my life: _____

A choice in my life: _____

Reflection on my search for this day: _____

_____

_____

_____

_____

DAY 3

Something important in my life: _____

An interesting corner of my life: _____

A token or symbol of my life: _____

A photograph of my life: _____

A choice in my life: _____

Reflection on my search for this day: _____

_____

_____

_____

_____

DAY 4

Something important in my life: _____

An interesting corner of my life: _____

A token or symbol of my life: _____

A photograph of my life: _____

A choice in my life: _____

Reflection on my search for this day: _____

_____

_____

_____

_____

DAY 5

Something important in my life: _____

An interesting corner of my life: _____

A token or symbol of my life: _____

A photograph of my life: _____

A choice in my life: _____

Reflection on my search for this day: _____

_____

_____

_____

_____

DAY 6

Something important in my life: _____

An interesting corner of my life: _____

A token or symbol of my life: _____

A photograph of my life: _____

A choice in my life: _____

Reflection on my search for this day: _____

_____

_____

_____

_____

DAY 7

Something important in my life: _____

An interesting corner of my life: _____

A token or symbol of my life: _____

A photograph of my life: _____

A choice in my life: _____

Reflection on my search for this day: _____

_____

_____

_____

_____

Answer these final questions only after you've completed all seven days of the exercise.

1. What have you learned about your life from this seven-day entry?

_____

_____

_____

_____

2. What have you learned about yourself?

_____

_____

_____

_____

3. How can you use this "self-portrait" to help open your eyes to fresh ideas in your life?

_____

_____

_____

_____

- Did you discover anything new and interesting about yourself? If you didn't, why not?
- Do you need to be more open to new ways of seeing and thinking? How can you bring a fresh perspective to your life?
- Was there anything disturbing about this entry? What was the most disturbing part?

Inner Relaxation

In many ways, contemplation is thought without action. It is a nonaction, the purpose of which is to relax and switch off that part of you that has to spring into action and take care of things. One goal of the process of contemplation *is* to guide and enable decision making. Solving problems and making important life decisions are least effective when they're simply knee-jerk reactions to what's going around you. Informed decisions and wise actions are more likely to result from relaxed contemplation than from stress, tension, and pressure.

Informed decisions and wise actions are more likely to result from relaxed contemplation than from stress, tension, and pressure.

In this respect, contemplation is tied to the ability to relax. There are many ways to relax, of course, and you had the opportunity to think about relaxation and health in Chapter 10. Some people relax by reading a book, others by sipping a glass of wine, and still others by running five miles or lifting weights. The point of relaxation is not to be motionless but to separate mind and body from emotional stress.

The previous journal entries helped stimulate your internal thought processes through your interactions with the world outside of you. The next entry focuses on the ability to think more clearly and effectively through deep internal relaxation. It builds on the process of "visualization," where you self-induce a relaxed state to free yourself of the burdens of your daily life. It's a way to refresh your body and mind. The written journal entry follows a relaxation and visualization experience. Turn to the entry immediately after completing the relaxation and visualization exercise presented here. You may wish to make a copy of the entry before completing it so that you can repeat the exercise another time. Plan to spend about fifteen minutes or longer on the exercise itself.

- Create a relaxing and comfortable environment. For instance, darken the room, light a fragrant candle, or play some quiet background music.

- Find a comfortable position that you can maintain for ten to fifteen minutes. Lying on your back with your hands by your sides is a good position for this exercise, but you can take any other position that is relaxing and natural for you. Begin the exercise, keeping your eyes closed the entire time.

- Relax each set of muscles in your body, one at a time, from your toes to your head. Start by tightly tensing your toes for just a moment, then gradually relax them. Allow the tension to move up into your feet and ankles, then relax that part of your body. Keep this wave of tension and relaxation moving through your body until every group of muscles is relaxed. The process takes about five minutes, but you can choose to take more time, if you'd like.

- Once physically relaxed, picture a favorite place in your life that has provided emotional comfort or warmth. You can visualize a quiet beach under a warm sun or a snow-covered mountaintop at dawn. You may prefer to choose a childhood spot associated with fond memories or a place connected to someone important in your life. Find an image that evokes reassuring feelings. This is your comfort image.

- Concentrate on this pleasant image. Imagine the feel of the sand, the smell of the grass, or other sensations and memories relevant to that image. Let these feelings wash over you. As you do, tune in to your body. Concentrate on steady, shallow breathing. Pay attention to the rhythm of your heart. Be aware of the position and weight of your head, arms, and legs.

◆ As thoughts of the day enter your mind, let them wash over and through you without emotion. If there's a dramatic or urgent feeling connected to these thoughts, screen them out by concentrating again on your comfort image. Continue to stay tuned in to your body as well. Feel the warmth of an imagined sun and the weight of your own body gently connecting you to everything around you. As you pass through the exercise, imagine you're floating weightlessly on a sea of air, with a cool breeze passing over you.

◆ Spend about ten minutes in this relaxed state. Once you feel ready to write, complete your journal entry, first describing the relaxation experience. The journal entry concludes with a freewriting exercise—putting pen to paper and writing whatever comes to mind.

There are many variations on relaxation and visualization exercises, and you can adapt them to fit your own needs. This is one version for you to experiment with. You can also buy prerecorded materials from any music store to guide you to inner relaxation as you listen to the tape or CD. Like many of the other journal entries, this one can be repeated many times.

INNER PEACE

1. What comfort image did you use in the visualization exercise?

_____

_____

_____

2. Why did you choose this image?

_____

_____

_____

3. Overall, what was the relaxation and visualization experience like?

_____

_____

_____

_____

_____

_____

4. Complete these sentences.

a. *Right now, I feel* . . . _____

_____

b. *At this moment, things in my life seem* . . . _____

_____

c. *Right now, the issue most on my mind is* . . . _____

_____

5. Take a few moments to write about anything that comes to mind.

_____

_____

_____

_____

_____

_____

_____

_____

_____

_____

_____

_____

_____

- Were you able to use this exercise to facilitate relaxation and contemplation? Did you find freewriting at the end of your journal entry easy or difficult? Was what you wrote—or didn't write—connected to the relaxation exercise?
- Is this an exercise that you'll repeat? Do you need to modify this exercise to better suit your own needs? If this form of relaxation wasn't helpful, are there other ways to relax that better fit your needs and style?
- Is it important to find a way to deeply relax each day? In what ways can relaxed contemplation help you think through issues more clearly?

Moving Forward with Fresh Eyes

If you've worked your way through *The Healing Journey Through Divorce,* by now your married life is moving into the past and your new life is already here or clearly looming ahead. As you make decisions about the rest of your life, it'll be important to do so with clear thinking and fresh ideas, many of which will be based on what you've learned from your divorce. Are you able to use the past to plan and build your future?

CHECKPOINT: NEW THINKING

1. What have you discovered about yourself?

_____

_____

_____

_____

_____

2. What have you discovered about your life?

_____

_____

_____

_____

3. What's important in your life now and ahead?

_____

_____

_____

_____

_____

4. What changes do you see ahead?

_____

_____

_____

_____

_____

5. What needs to be left behind?

_____

_____

_____

_____

6. Where do you go from here?

_____

_____

_____

_____

THINGS TO THINK ABOUT

- Is looking "inside" something that can help your decision-making process? Do you need to find ways or the time to be more contemplative?
- How can you best use new eyes to apply fresh ideas to thinking about and planning your future?

14

Destination:

REINVENTING YOURSELF

KATE

It took me years to really recover from my divorce. In a way, not much changed after Paul left. Although he got involved with someone else right away, my life was pretty much the same. I still had the kids, the same home, and the same tasks of everyday life.

It took me a long time to realize I could have a new life too. Actually, it took me a long time to accept that I could have a new life, and do something about it. Paul provided a decent amount of money to take care of the kids, and that actually gave me the chance to do things a little differently myself. I started with some adult education classes, and later went back to school full-time. Getting a new career was not only liberating but gave me a sense of empowerment too. Although I was still unsure of myself, I could tell that others were seeing me as competent and bright, and that was pretty reassuring. Dating wasn't much fun, but it got me back into the world, and in the end I decided that friendships were probably more important than finding the next "right" partner. Little by little, my self-image was changing and I found myself leaving the old feelings behind and getting on with my life.

I still don't like Paul, but I like myself a whole lot better.

THE FINAL STAGES of any divorce involve picking up and rebuilding. This doesn't mean forgetting the past and all you've been through, but it does mean moving forward, unfettered by the issues of the past. People who can't detach themselves from their past are likely to feel continually traumatized by it. They remain stuck in their ability to express and eventually let go of feelings, free themselves of an old self-image, and personally grow in ways they perhaps never imagined.

To lead a successful and satisfying life after divorce means the complete acceptance of your divorce and all the changes it has brought.

To lead a successful and satisfying life after divorce means the complete acceptance of your divorce and all the changes it has brought and the acceptance of the personal responsibility required to build new relationships of all kinds, new interests, and a new life. The past is a prologue to what's ahead. You can prevent it from ruining your present and use it to build your future. In this chapter you'll have the opportunity to think about what it means to reinvent yourself.

The Choice to Change

Choice is a relative thing. Sometimes your choices are wide open, restricted only by your imagination and your will, but other times they are defined or limited by your circumstances. It's not always easy to realize you have choices, but you do. For one thing, *how* you live your life is a choice. Starting from that point, you make many other choices. Although current circumstances can prevent immediate choice, people are still able to work toward change over time. You may be limited by many real-life constraints but that doesn't mean you can't make choices. In the final analysis, accepting responsibility for your life means recognizing that you do have choices, even if you *choose* not to exercise them.

You may be limited by many real-life constraints but that doesn't mean you can't make choices.

Reinvention is a way of saying that you have a choice about how you want to live your life, within your own particular circumstances, and about the kind of person you decide to be now and in the future. Personal reinvention, though, is not simply about choices; it's about *identity* and, specifically, how you see yourself.

The "background" to your daily life and experience of the world, and in many important aspects your identity, is largely defined by four major components.

1. *Vocational choices* are the things you do that, in part, define your identity, such as occupation, school, volunteer work, homemaking, and so on.

2. *Social activities* are the personal activities in which you engage.

3. *Relationships* include all people in whom you invest your personal energy and time, whether platonically or romantically.

4. *Lifestyle* is an aspect of your identity that includes where and how you live and the tasks and responsibilities of your everyday life.

Some of these things may be unchangeable or at least highly resistant to change. Your daily responsibilities, for instance, may be defined by your role as a parent or caregiver. Although you can't stop being a caregiver, you can change at least some of the circumstances that affect your life and ability to make choices.

Use the following journal entry to create an inventory of the changes you'd like to make in your life and to begin exploring the possibility of change.

Reinvention is a way of saying that you have a choice about how you want to live your life, within your own particular circumstances, and about the kind of person you decide to be now and in the future.

AN INVENTORY OF CHANGE

1. Complete these sentences.

a. *In my current life, I'm* most *satisfied with* . . . _____

_____

b. *In my current life, I'm* least *satisfied with* . . . _____

_____

c. *I would most like to change* . . . _____

_____

d. *I wish I could* . . . _____

_____

2. Consider your current vocation.

a. How satisfied are you? _____

_____

b. Are there changes you'd like to make? _____

_____

c. What stops you from making changes? _____

_____

3. Consider your social activities.

a. How satisfied are you? _____

_____

b. Are there changes you'd like to make? _____

_____

c. What stops you from making changes? _____

_____

4. Consider your relationships.

a. How satisfied are you? _____

_____

b. Are there changes you'd like to make? _____

_____

c. What stops you from making changes? _____

_____

5. Consider your lifestyle.

a. How satisfied are you? _____

_____

b. Are there changes you'd like to make? _____

_____

c. What stops you from making changes? _____

_____

6. Check off the areas of your life that are most in need of a "makeover," and add ideas of your own.

__career   __income   __physical health

__day-to-day work   __living situation   __relationships, family

__education   __personal interests __relationships, platonic

__housing   __physical appearance __relationships, romantic

other: _____   _____

_____   _____

_____   _____

7. How important is it for you to make changes or improve on any of these areas in your life? Why?

_____

_____

_____

_____

_____

THINGS TO THINK ABOUT

- Are the changes you want realistic, given the circumstances of your life?
- Do you have the necessary resources in your life to bring about changes you'd like to make? If not, how can you develop such resources?
- Who else will be affected by any changes you might make? In what ways?

New Roads to Travel

Can you see an opportunity to take a different fork in the road? Are there forks in the road that you're just not seeing? Are there new interests waiting to be discovered? Part of your healing journey is the exploration of new roads that have no painful associations with past events. As always, if you're a custodial parent you may have to choose roads that are practical for you and your children to follow now, deferring others until a later date. Perhaps you'll turn back, not liking where the road is leading you. Or maybe you will discover a whole new set of roads that you never imagined were there or available to you.

Discovery, however, usually requires some vision. Most explorers set out to discover something they suspect exists; they don't set out hoping to stumble across just anything. Having some vision of where you'd like your roads to lead can provide you with some direction. Whichever route you choose to take, there are likely to be consequences of some kind. You may feel unsure of yourself in new territory or completely uprooted. You may feel less competent as you take on a new role or identity or insecure as you push forward into new relationships or a new job.

The journal entries that follow will help you to focus broadly on change in your life, what change might be required from you, and what prevents change. The next entry focuses on just one area of possible change. Look back at the areas of desired change you identified in the previous journal entry. Pick any one of the areas you'd like to improve on or change in some way, and focus only on this area in the next entry. Copy the blank entry first so that you can use it to explore other avenues of change.

MAKEOVER

1. Which aspect of your life will you focus on?

_____

_____

2. What is most dissatisfying about this part of your life?

_____

_____

_____

_____

_____

3. What would you most like to change about this part of your life?

_____

_____

_____

_____

_____

4. What must you do to make a change or bring about an improvement?

_____

_____

_____

_____

_____

5. What are the possible risks of change in this area?

_____

_____

_____

_____

_____

6. What do you stand to gain by making a change in this area?

_____

_____

_____

_____

7. What resources will you need to bring about change in this area?

_____

_____

_____

_____

8. Whose personal support will be most important in making this change?

_____

_____

_____

_____

9. Who else will be affected by changes you make in this area? In what ways?

_____

_____

_____

_____

THINGS TO THINK ABOUT

- Do you really want to change this area of your life? What might you lose by making a change?
- What personal doubts or fears hold you back?
- Who can you turn to for help? Do you most need your natural support system or your drafted support system to effect this change? (You may wish to review Chapter 6 before considering your answers.)

Thinking About New Relationships

The last chapter helped you explore your current relationships and what you want from them. Many of your new relationships may be an outgrowth of old or existing ones.

Though people from your former life who are now part of your new life are probably playing different roles, your attitude about those relationships may still be shaped by past expectations, disappointments, and successes.

At the same time, new relationships are developing and you're making decisions about the sort of relationships you want. Of course, wanting something and getting it are two different matters. It's important to realize that regardless of how much you may want or need a particular relationship not every pursuit is successful. But don't let fear of failure or disappointment keep you from the pursuit. As the Roman statesman Seneca once noted, "To keep oneself safe does not mean to bury oneself."

Relationships fall into four primary categories: family, friends, colleagues, and romantic partners.

Relationships fall into four primary categories: family, friends, colleagues, and romantic partners. Sometimes a relationship of one type turns into another. A sibling can become a close friend. A coworker can become a lover. Of these four types of relationships, family is the least likely to radically change, but even so relationships can evolve. Your former in-laws, for instance, may remain in your life but in a different role or set of interactions.

But before thinking about new relationships, take a moment to think about yourself. Whether you were married for two years or thirty-two years, you're not the same person you were when you first married. Living and sharing your life with someone has affected your emotions, responses, and interests, among other things.

This journal entry will help you to identify who you are now. It raises questions that you should continue to bear in mind as you pursue and enter into new relationships.

WHO AM I NOW?

1. Who was I before my marriage?

_____

_____

_____

2. In what ways has my marriage changed me?

_____

_____

_____

3. In what ways has my divorce changed me?

_____

_____

_____

_____

4. Who am I now?

_____

_____

_____

a. *I am . . .* _____

b. *I am . . .* _____

c. *I am . . .* _____

d. *I am . . .* _____

THINGS TO THINK ABOUT

- Can you discern a difference between the ways your marriage changed you and the way your divorce changed you?
- In what ways are you still changing?

Exploring New Relationships

Relationships are like jigsaw puzzles. To be successful and have your needs met, the pieces must match and fit together.

What do you want from new relationships? Although the next entry will help you to think about what kind of relationships you want at this time in your life, keep in mind that there's more to successful relationships than simply identifying your desires. Relationships are like jigsaw puzzles. To be successful and have your needs met, the pieces must match and fit together. Unsuccessful relationships are often the result of mismatched parts or parts that have been forced together.

As you move out into the world, you're almost certain to be faced with the prospect of sexual relationships. Some people feel liberated after their divorce and want to engage in sexual relationships freely and often. Others are more cautious or see sex as a form of intimacy reserved for only the most special of relationships. Still others are simply not interested in or ready for another sexual relationship after their divorce. Eventually, though, you're probably going to be faced with wanting sex or someone wanting sex with you. This is just one more facet of your new life as a single person. The next journal entry will help you to think about the complexities of relationships in general and allow you the opportunity to think before you act, understand your needs, and reflect on the lessons of past relationships in the development of new ones.

REINVENTING RELATIONSHIPS

1. Complete these sentences.

a. *In my relationships, I want . . .* _____

_____

b. *I really want a relationship that can . . .* _____

_____

c. *I most need my relationships to . . .* _____

_____

d. *When I think of new relationships, I . . .* _____

_____

e. *In any new relationship, I worry that . . .* _____

_____

2. What sort of relationships do you most want in your life right now?

_____

_____

_____

_____

3. What sort of relationships do you most need?

_____

_____

_____

4. What sort of relationships are you ready for?

_____

_____

_____

5. Are you ready for, or do you want, sexual relationships? If so, what kind: romantic and intimate, casual and temporary, or permanent and committed?

_____

_____

6. What are your greatest barriers to new relationships?

_____

_____

_____

_____

7. In what ways can you help build new relationships?

_____

_____

_____

_____

8. How can you be best prepared for new relationships that don't work out the way you hoped or aren't meeting your needs?

_____

_____

_____

9. What have you learned from past relationships that help you figure out what you want, and what to avoid, from developing relationships?

a. *What I've learned about myself is* . . . _____

_____

_____

_____

_____

b. *What I've learned about others is* . . . _____

_____

_____

_____

_____

THINGS TO THINK ABOUT

- What sort of relationships should you most focus on now? Are there certain kinds of relationships to avoid at this time in your life?
- Do you know what to avoid as you build or seek new relationships? Are you wiser from the experience of your divorce?
- Are you doing enough to build new relationships, or are you waiting for them to "happen" to you? Are you going to the right places and doing the right things? How do you know what the "right" things are?

Building New Relationships

Use the next entry to focus on specific relationships. The format is open; you can use the entry to reflect on any kind of developing relationship interest, from platonic to purely sexual to romantic. Use the entry to explore different current relationships and your relationship needs and interests as they develop and change over time.

WHAT I WANT

1. Who's the subject of this entry?

_____

2. What sort of relationship are you describing?

_____

_____

_____

3. Is the relationship satisfying as it is?

_____

_____

_____

4. What sort of relationship do you want?

_____

_____

_____

5. What don't you want from this relationship?

_____

_____

_____

6. How can you most help the relationship along?

_____

_____

_____

_____

7. What are your greatest fears about this relationship or about your own behavior?

_____

_____

_____

8. What behaviors or mistakes should you avoid?

_____

_____

_____

_____

_____

9. What's the best way to handle this relationship?

_____

_____

_____

_____

_____

10. How will you react if this relationship fails to meet your needs or disappoints you in other ways?

_____

_____

_____

_____

_____

THINGS TO THINK ABOUT

- Are you being realistic about this relationship? Can it succeed? Should it succeed?
- Are you picking the right person for this relationship? Are you repeating old mistakes or correcting them?
- Does this person share your feelings or know how you feel? Have you discussed your feelings with him or her? Should you reveal your feelings?
- Do you have a friend or confidant with whom you can share your feelings and fears about this relationship, and get advice if needed?

Preparing to Move On

As you complete this chapter, you're pretty much in the final throes of your divorce work. If you're working on the major changes your new life requires and ready for the development of meaningful new relationships, you've actively taken on the tasks and challenges of this final stage—the re-formation of your life.

This isn't to say that you no longer have feelings, regrets, or unfinished business about your marriage. The point that marks the end of divorce work is not forgiving or forgetting—you may never feel either way. On the contrary, you may continue to have strong feelings off and on for years to come. It would be strange if you didn't have ongoing feelings about such an important part of your life. It isn't the end of feelings that signals the successful completion of your divorce work, but instead your ability to bear your feelings without being unduly burdened by them and to manage them without their negatively interfering with your life.

CHECKPOINT: REINVENTION

1. As you reinvent your life, what lessons must you apply to your:

a. relationships?_____

_____

b. lifestyle? _____

_____

c. decision-making style?_____

_____

2. What past mistakes and pitfalls are to be avoided in your:

a. relationships?_____

_____

b. lifestyle? _____

_____

c. decision-making style?_____

_____

3. What have you most learned from your marriage?

_____

_____

_____

4. What have you most learned from your divorce?

_____

_____

_____

_____

_____

THINGS TO THINK ABOUT

- Were you able to distinguish lessons learned from your marriage from lessons learned from your divorce? Did Questions 3 and 4 seem like the same question?
- Are you ready to move on with life after divorce? Do you need to do more divorce work before making decisions about new relationships? What kind of help or support might you need in reinventing your life?

15

Destination:

MOVING ON

WILLIAM

My life's very different now. I got custody of our two girls after the divorce and changed my whole lifestyle almost at once. I knew how responsible I had to be now, and I took on a whole new attitude. I still worked hard, but I also spent more time with the girls. I started thinking differently about the kind of life I wanted and needed now. Even though things got nasty with Jennifer sometimes, especially over the girls, I never let it pull me in. I just kept thinking about how to move my new life along without getting caught up in the old stuff.

Life did change over the next few years. I'm remarried, with a couple of stepkids, and have a new child as well. Between me and my new wife, we do well with all our kids and enjoy the life we live together. In a way, I have my old life to thank for my new life.

AS YOU CERTAINLY know by now, you may never fully resolve all of the things you've felt, and probably still feel with respect to your divorce. These emotions may come back to haunt you over the years. But the issues that are directly ahead involve how to immerse yourself in your new life as a single person. The goals of this final stage most fully involve your ability to move on with your life, unrestrained by old feelings.

By now you've probably fallen back into a daily routine of some kind, and most people expect you to be pretty much over the major issues and disruptions of your divorce. At this point in your divorce work this is a reasonable expectation. If divorce issues are still actively interfering with your daily life, then you probably shouldn't be working in this chapter. Your divorce work should have taken you through many of the steps required to be able to function effectively once again, and you should be prepared to focus on the *rest* of your life.

Decisions about Your Future

No doubt you're limited by many real-life constraints—finances, relationships, jobs, and other matters over which you don't necessarily have full control. These make up the backdrop of your life against which decisions are made. Often, there's more than one "correct" decision, and more than one "wrong" choice. But there are certainly guides to decision making that can help you to think about and arrive at if not the "right" decision, then an appropriate one. As you think about decisions and your choices, consider these three factors.

1. *Responsibility*. Some decisions are not really choices at all; they are requirements, especially when attached to personal responsibility. If you're a parent, for instance, you have decisions that must be made to ensure the welfare of your children. But in reality, even such requirements can be ducked by those unwilling to accept their responsibilities. Consider "dead-beat parents," for example, who try to dodge making support payments for their children. As you plan your future, think about who will be affected by your decisions and for whom you may be responsible.

2. *Spontaneity versus impetuousness*. Sometimes there's no reason in the world not to act on a whim. It's healthy to be spontaneous at times. Where spontaneity is generally thought of

as harmless and even refreshing, we usually think of impetuous behavior as thoughtless and potentially problematic. As you make decisions, think about the difference between being spontaneous and being impetuous.

3. *Long-Term effects*. Take into account that decisions you make now may have effects in the long run. Buying a new wardrobe of clothes, seeking a new career, or moving from one home to another in the same community may involve some deep decision making, but none represent necessarily radical changes. On the other hand, selling your home and moving to another state, giving permanent custody of your children to your ex-spouse, or giving up your job are far more significant decisions in terms of their long-term impact, and they are often difficult decisions to reverse later.

As you make decisions, think about the difference between being spontaneous and being impetuous.

Your current situation has opened up the possibility of change, but be careful. Decisions are powerful things because they shape the things that follow. Use this next journal entry to think about change, decisions, and the consequences of choices you might be considering.

THINKING ABOUT DECISIONS

1. Think about current decisions and choices in your life. What sort of decisions are the hardest to make?

_____

_____

_____

_____

2. In what way has your divorce led to the sort of choices you're facing?

_____

_____

_____

3. In what ways has your divorce opened up your life to the possibility of change?

_____

_____

_____

_____

4. What sort of opportunities for change are in your life right now?

_____

_____

_____

_____

_____

5. What are the risks of change?

_____

_____

_____

_____

_____

6. Who else might be affected by your decisions? In what ways?

_____

_____

_____

_____

_____

THINGS TO THINK ABOUT

- Are you afraid of change or excited by it? Do your fears about change outweigh the opportunities?
- Are you at a point in your life where you can spot opportunity for change? What can you do to increase your ability to see such opportunities?

Moving Forward

By now your new living situation postdivorce has become permanent. As you plan for your future, there are steps that can help you to arrive at decisions appropriate for your lifestyle and responsibilities.

- Recognize that you do have choices. You're not simply a passive agent of the way things "have" to be.

- Consider the nature of the problem that you're trying to resolve. Every decision is a *response* to a particular situation: what's the issue, problem, or situation you want to address?

- Consider all your options, even the outlandish ones. Be creative.

- Evaluate your choices. Determine which choices you can realistically make right now. If you are left with only one option, your decision might be made.

- Consider all consequences. What are the downsides to your possible decisions? Who will be affected by your choice, and how? How will your possible choices affect your life, your finances, your relationships, and so on?

- Reflect on your decision. What will it feel like to actually take those steps and make that choice? What will it feel like if you reject that choice? Is the decision you're pondering permanent or is it reversible?

The next journal entry is intended to help you think about individual choices and your decision-making style in general. Copy the blank format if you think you may want to repeat the entry to think through the same choice from more than one perspective or to consider other decisions. Follow the general model for decision making described above. This is a framework you can use to map out solutions for almost any issue in your life.

MAKING DECISIONS

1. Briefly describe one decision you're currently pondering.

_____

2. Name at least six different choices for resolving this issue.

_____   _____

_____   _____

_____   _____

3. Review the options you've just identified, and select the three most rational and realistic choices. Under each, describe how this choice could fit the circumstances and reality of your life.

a. *This solution fits because . . .* _____

b. *This solution fits because . . .* _____

c. *This solution fits because . . .* _____

4. Now select just one of these choices, and use it as the focal point for the remainder of this entry.

_____

5. What are possible consequences of this choice? Is there a price to pay?

_____

_____

_____

6. How will your life be affected by this choice?

_____

_____

_____

_____

7. Who else's life will be affected by this decision, and how?

_____

_____

_____

_____

_____

THINGS TO THINK ABOUT

- Do you better understand the issues and choices involved in this decision? What stops you from making a choice and acting on it in this case?
- Can you afford to take a chance on this decision, or are the consequences irreversible?
- Are you acting too quickly on decisions without giving them ample thought, or are you not proceeding quickly enough?

The Past as Prologue

What can you carry from your marriage and all it has taught you? The ability to draw from your past and use it as a source of comfort and strength is a difficult task, but once accomplished it marks the point at which you have left your divorce work behind and can step into your future. Those who haven't learned from the past risk repeating past mistakes. Your past is the prologue to your future.

Part of moving on is letting go—an enormously difficult task. Failing to let go of an anchor can pull you down with it. As you think about the past, focus on all it's given you rather than all it may have taken. Before you complete your next entry, consider this thought:

The ability to draw from your past and use it as a source of comfort and strength is a difficult task, but once accomplished it marks the point at which you have left your divorce work behind and can step into your future.

The past, with its pleasures, its rewards, its foolishness, its punishments, is there for each of us forever, and it should be.
——LILLIAN HELLMAN

INSTRUCTION FROM THE PAST

1. What did your marriage teach you about life?

_____

_____

_____

_____

_____

2. What did your marriage teach you about love?

_____

_____

_____

_____

_____

3. What did your marriage teach you about relationships?

_____

_____

_____

_____

_____

4. What did your marriage teach you about yourself?

_____

_____

_____

_____

_____

5. Complete these sentences.

a. *My marriage was fertile ground for me because . . .* _____

_____

b. *My marriage allowed me . . .* _____

_____

c. *In my marriage, I most appreciate . . .* _____

_____

d. *In my marriage, I most regret . . .* _____

_____

6. What has your divorce taught you?

_____

_____

_____

_____

_____

_____

THINGS TO THINK ABOUT

- Reviewing what you've just written, are you ready to move ahead with your new life? Do you need to do more divorce work before making major life decisions?
- Are you ready to let go of feelings that will only drag and keep you down? If not, where and how can you get some help in learning how to let go?
- What does letting go mean to you? Is it the same as forgiving or forgetting, or is it a different concept?

Handling the Future

The future will contain its fair share of bumps. Proceeding with your life and learning from the past means moving forward with eyes wide open.

There are many issues connected to your divorce that you'll continue to deal with in the future. Some of these problems and issues may already be developing; others you may be able to predict.

Your divorce work has helped you deal with the emotional, practical, and personal issues that you've faced since the initial decision to divorce. These are skills you can apply to every facet of your life as you deal with issues now developing, or as yet unforeseen.

There are many resources available to help you deal with the practical, emotional, and other aspects of divorce. But if you've found your divorce journal to be useful, return to it often. As issues, feelings, questions, and problems emerge over time, turn to your journal as a source for quiet reflection and personal development.

Take a few moments to think about your long journey. Then complete the next journal entry.

REFLECTIONS ON YOUR JOURNEY

1. *I've learned . . .* _____

_____

_____

_____

_____

_____

_____

_____

2. *As I look back on my divorce work, I . . .* _____

_____

_____

_____

_____

_____

_____

_____

3. My divorce journey has left me feeling . . . _____

_____

_____

_____

_____

_____

_____

4. The most bitter part of my journey has been . . . _____

_____

_____

_____

_____

_____

_____

5. The sweetest part of my journey has been . . . _____

_____

_____

_____

_____

_____

_____

_____

6. I most look forward to . . . _____

_____

_____

_____

_____

_____

_____

_____

THINGS TO THINK ABOUT

- Was this a difficult entry? Has this entry helped you to realize you're ready to complete your divorce work or that you still have a way to go?
- Is it okay to move forward with your life and still be doing divorce work? Does divorce work ever *have* to end?
- What has this journey most taught you about yourself and your life in general?

16

As One Journey Ends, Another Begins

Look not mournfully into the Past. It comes not back again. Wisely improve the Present. It is thine. Go forth to meet the shadowy Future, without fear . . .
—HENRY WADSWORTH LONGFELLOW

THE END OF this journal marks the end of your divorce work. But as you reach this point, you've really only completed one step in a lifelong journey. What you've been through and what you've learned through your journaling work sets the pace for the journey that's ahead.

If your journey has strengthened and nourished you, you're well on your way to defining and taking hold of your own future and best interests. You are a phoenix risen from the ashes of a lost relationship. If, however, your journey has left you emotionally shaky and uncertain, consider getting help. Individual counseling is one useful vehicle for exploring life issues. Divorce support groups offer a cooperative, communal, and sensitive environment for sharing and interacting with others in similar situations. There are other sources of assistance, such as counselors, therapists, and pastoral counselors. Of course, you don't have to be experiencing emotional difficulties to get help dealing with unresolved issues, uncertainties, and life decisions. Counseling and support groups are nurturing environments for people with many different needs.

Where will your life take you now? If you've used your divorce journal through this difficult time, then you've no doubt

Divorce support groups offer a cooperative, communal, and sensitive environment for sharing and interacting with others in similar situations.

found it useful and it may have served many purposes: a place to express or explore feelings, or both. Will your journal continue to be a useful tool and valuable companion as you continue along your lifelong journey? This final journal entry will help you to answer this question.

MY JOURNAL

1. How has your journal been most useful?

_____

_____

_____

_____

2. What's been the most difficult aspect of journaling for you?

_____

_____

_____

_____

3. What's been the most fulfilling aspect of journaling?

_____

_____

_____

_____

4. Overall, describe your experience keeping this journal.

_____

_____

_____

_____

5. My journal . . . _____

_____

_____

_____

_____

_____

_____

_____

_____

_____

_____

THINGS TO THINK ABOUT

- Have you enjoyed keeping a journal? If you've kept a journal before, what was different about this journal?
- Will you continue to use a journal in the future? If so, will you write in it only under special circumstances, or will you keep a daily journal?

In completing this book you've accomplished a great deal and taken significant steps down the path to healing, self-help, and personal growth. As your personal journey continues, the lessons and methods learned in this book will help you along the way.

Helpful Books

Ackerman, M. J. *Does Wednesday Mean Mom's House or Dad's?* New York: John Wiley & Sons, 1997.

American Bar Association. *Guide to Family Law*. New York: Times Books, 1996.

Bonkowski, S. (1990). *Teens Are Nondivorceable: A Workbook for Divorced Parents and Their Children*. Chicago, Ill.: ACTA Publications.

Cohen, S. K. (1980). *Whoever Said Life Is Fair? Growing Through Life's Injustices*. New York: Charles Scribner's Sons.

Condrell, K. N., with L. L. Small. *Be a Great Divorced Dad*. New York: St. Martin's Press, 1997.

Newman, G. *101 Ways to Be a Long-Distance Super-Dad*. Mountain View, Calif: Blossom Valley Press, 1981.

Schilling, E., III, and C. A. Wilson. *The Survival Manual for Men in Divorce*. Dubuque, Iowa: Kendall/Hunt, 1994.

Schwartz, L. L., and F. W. Kaslow. *Painful Partings: Divorce and Its Aftermath*. New York: John Wiley & Sons, 1997.

Shahan, L. *Living Alone and Liking It*. New York: Warner Books, 1988.

Teyber, E. *Helping Children Cope with Divorce*. San Francisco: Jossey-Bass, 1992.

About the Authors

PHIL RICH, EdD, MSW, holds a doctorate in applied behavioral and organizational studies and is a clinical social worker diplomate with a master's degree in social work. Over the past two decades, he has worked as a director of treatment programs, a clinical supervisor, and a practicing therapist. He is currently actively involved with inpatient care at the Brattleboro Retreat, and maintains a private outpatient practice in western Massachusetts.

LITA LINZER SCHWARTZ, PhD, ABPP (Forensic), is Distinguished Professor Emerita at the Pennsylvania State University. She has written, edited, or coauthored more than fifteen books previously, including *Painful Partings: Divorce and its Aftermath* (Wiley), *Mid-Life Divorce Counseling, The Dynamics of Divorce, Why Give Gifts to the Gifted?*, and *Alternatives to Infertility*, as well as more than ninety articles and chapters.

Acknowledgments

OUR THANKS TO Kelly Franklin, associate publisher at John Wiley & Sons. Kelly connected the two of us on this project and provided direction throughout. Kelly's role in the Healing Journey series is critical, and we thank her very much.

We also express our mutual appreciation to one another for those experiences and skills we each contributed to this joint effort. Although hundreds of miles apart, we managed to work well as partners.

From Lita: My thanks to Arthur, Joshua, and Frederic who help me on *all* my journeys and lead me on some very interesting roads.

From Phil: As always, my thanks and appreciation to Bev, and a very special thank you to my daughter, Kaye, who is the most delightful person I've ever known.